It's my party and I'll

knit if I want to!

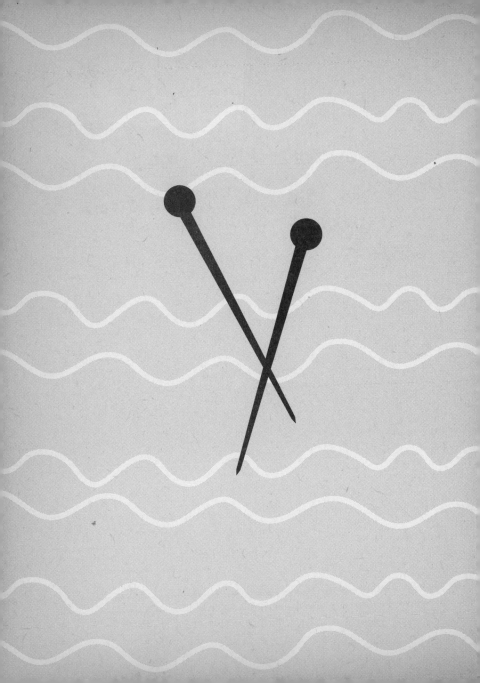

It's my party and I'll knit if I want to!

Sharon Aris

ALLEN&UNWIN

First published in 2003

Copyright © Sharon Aris 2003
Appendix is copyright © Patons 2002

Allen & Unwin
83 Alexander Street
Crows Nest NSW 2065
Australia
Phone: (61 2) 8425 0100
Fax: (61 2) 9906 2218
Email: info@allenandunwin.com
Web: www.allenandunwin.com

National Library of Australia
Cataloguing-in-Publication entry:

Aris, Sharon.
  It's my party and I'll knit if I want to!

  ISBN 1 74114 073 0.

  1. Knitting - Social aspects - Australia. 2. Women -
  Australia - Social life and customs. I. Title.

746.4320994

Design by Ellie Exarchos
Illustrations by Neryl Walker
Photographs by Wayne Fogden
Set in 10.35/16 pt Sabon by Bookhouse, Sydney
Printed Griffin Press, South Australia

10 9 8 7 6 5 4

Contents

About the author

Sharon Aris is a writer, television producer and knitter, not necessarily in that order. She lives in Sydney with her husband, Rob, and their cat, Crouching Tiger. She collects degrees of ephemera (Medieval Studies) and great seriousness (Applied Sociology) and has a fondness for margaritas. This is her second book.

It's my party and I'll **knit** if I want to!

CHAPTER ONE

Knitting is the new feminism

Q. *I have always been told that knitting was a private activity, best confined to one's home. However, recently I have noticed several young women knitting in common social situations. Is it now acceptable for me to knit in public?*

A. Manners, as always, dictate all public behaviour and a few basic considerations will ensure your public knitting is undisturbed. Solo knitting, while on the train or in the park at lunchtime is a pleasant activity that most enjoy watching. In mixed social company however, it is polite to ask, 'Do you mind if I knit?' while assuming, as do most smokers, the answer will be affirmative. However, at business meetings, weddings and funerals public knitting sends a quiet message of indifference, so it is best refrained from unless that particular point is to be made.

Knitting Diary, July 2001

At Sunday afternoon barbecue my friend Joanne announces that she is knitting a jumper. I laugh. How eccentric. Joanne is 33 and a lobbyist in Canberra.

Knitting Diary, August 2001

At weekday lunch mirthfully regale friend Tiffany, 32, with Joanne's obscure pastime. Joke falls flat when Tiffany says breezily, 'Oh, I knit. Have since my teens.' Tiffany runs her own small business.

Knitting Diary, September 2001

Birthday drinks with Eva, 33, who mentions she has organised a knitting class with her work colleagues. Eva is a community programs manager.

Am deeply suspicious. Something is going on. What is possessing my friends? All are 30-something, high achieving, overworking career girls. Knitting is traditional, ridiculously time consuming, manual labour, daggy and highly repetitious. Are they having a career crisis? Are they bored? Is it just a fad? Or is it something more? I must investigate.

'It's a sensuous thing,' says Joanne, 'I can feel the wool and know what I'm going to make just by holding the skeins.'

'It's something unique,' says Eva, 'Not mass-produced.'

'I like to be able to say my child wears hand-made jumpers,' says Tiffany.

Tiffany Hutton, 34, is a book editor, small business operator and a mother of two. Tiff figured out early that knitting was radical: 'I was a very rebellious teenager and it seemed so deviant,' she says with a grin, 'no-one else knitted. I used to knit in my French class. My teacher called me Madame Defarge.' Madame Defarge knitted from a revolutionary box seat beside the guillotine while heads rolled in Charles Dickens' *A Tale of Two Cities.*

Tiffany has her own theories as to why she likes something so traditional as knitting: 'When I'm working—editing—I'm thinking about other people's stuff,' she says. 'When I knit, that's mine. I like to be able to say, "I work, I have a job, I have a brain and I hand-knit jumpers."'

Tiffany grew up in Singapore and retains a particular expatriate air of doing things properly. 'I don't know if this is too simplistic or determinist,' she continues from her work studio at the back of her house, 'but I think it's possible that some women have found climbing the corporate ladder has not provided enough sense of creation.'

'And,' she says, 'I do think that last generation's feminism did undervalue "women's work". Now we are coming to an age when we remember fondly the things our mothers or grandmothers would do for us—cook, sew, knit, whatever— and perhaps we think there's no reason we can't do these things as well.'

So Tiffany is reclaiming the domestic arts. But strictly on her own terms. 'There's plenty of women who feel ripped off that the 50/50 partnership with your husband in work and domestic things hasn't happened,' she says, 'but instead of just being angry, its nice to make something of it.' For Tiffany, this means embracing the fun domestic stuff—cooking, knitting, time with her kids—and outsourcing invisible things, like scrubbing the bathroom, to a cleaner. The point is choosing which ones she'll do.

'I don't consider myself any less a feminist because I can cook, knit and keep a good house. In fact, I feel a little sorry for those women who think that in order to be "successful" they have to reject these skills. Reject anything exclusively associated with the female world,' she says. 'I like reclaiming those skills.'

I like that. Knitting is the old-new feminism. It's about having something more than a career. It's about digging the archaeology of our pasts and finding the baby that got thrown out with the feminist bathwater. It's looking for a state of grace in our lives. It's feminism for women who really want it all, not just a career, not just to stay home.

The big lie, the glamorous career. By the time we hit our thirties we find out that a job, even when it is fun, is just a job. Terribly useful when it comes to paying for holidays, shoes, the rent, food, that sort of thing, but it's not really the stuff of soul. In the back of our minds is this nagging question: when we decided to throw our lot in with careers and to hell with everything else, did we lose something?

If you think about it, it makes sense. Why wouldn't we concentrate on the home front? It is, after all, where our life's biggest business is conducted. Unlike our forerunners in the sisterhood, the nitty-gritty, pointy end of our negotiations are happening at home: you support my career, I'll support yours. I'll cook tonight, you wash up. I'll take this year off with the kids, you take next. All of a sudden we've started to get homey. We cook. We can garden. We entertain. Maybe knitting is radical after all. Home is where it's at. This is the third wave for feminism: first it was getting to work, then it was getting to the top, now it is getting a life.

I try that idea out on Danni Townsend, 33, a film director and journalist. 'I took up knitting as something to talk about besides career,' she agrees. Danni is, without any question, a go-getting gal. A classic type-A personality with tight curls and a Cupid face. 'In fact, it was like an antidote to my career,' she continues. 'I was working on a short film for six months and it felt like it would never be finished. It got to a point when I was getting frustrated with how long things were taking me in my career. I had a friend who was knitting and I thought, that's something I can finish.'

One scarf led to another, then a jumper, then another scarf. Now Danni's film is finished, but she's still knitting. She hasn't dumped the career, she's doing something more. And while she hasn't crossed the knitting-in-public bridge, she says there is a fearlessness to knitting. 'I don't knit in public,' she says, 'but I don't make it a secret either. It does take on this funny old-ladyness. I think you do reach an age where you think, fuck it, who cares?'

'There is something about wanting to create,' she says, thinking further, 'wanting to make things. It's like the growers' markets that are becoming popular, things are home-grown.

With knitting there's a real pride and satisfaction. I picked the wool, I made it. A real pride in having been able to do it.'

Maybe knitting is like a whole lot of old-fashioned skills more connected to the earth, to creativity, not a machine. After all, the average professional spends up to ten hours a day in front of a computer producing work that only exists in dots and dashes. Actually making something tangible holds great appeal. And it makes watching television productive.

Lisa Herrod is 31 and a newish knitter. We're meeting for lunch at one of those trendy-cosy cafés better known to locals than tourists. Set away from the main drag and on the wrong side of the street; you have to be told about Café Zoe, you're unlikely to just stumble across it. Meeting here, eating here, gives you a feeling of intimacy. It's packed, from its dark banquettes to the tables jostling on the polished grey-brown concrete floor.

An exceptionally groovy chick who drives a pink Holden, Lisa is someone I have met once before, but at first I don't recognise her. When she's with her social group Lisa fills a room. She's part mother-hen, part agent provocateur and part artist. Her personal website is called 'bunnyboiler'. She works as website designer, web teacher and interpreter for the deaf.

But sitting alone at the table she's small with an almost delicate air.

'Why did you take up knitting?' I ask.

'It was on my list,' she says, opening her eyes a little wide.

'What list?' I press.

'I had a list of things I wanted to do,' she says in an 'everyone-has-one-don't-they?' tone. 'Knitting is just one of the things.'

'I wrote it two or three years ago and recently I was sitting at work, I pulled it out of my drawer and there was knitting. So I got a book—I found it second-hand at a market—and I taught myself to knit. How to cast on, knit, purl, and that was it.'

Lisa is now collecting eccentric old knitting patterns: 'I've got this old wartime pattern for covering plaster casts,' she gestures to a mock-broken leg. 'The woman's one has an extra hole for the heel.' Her next obsession is tortoiseshell knitting needles. And then there are bigger plans. 'On my list I want to get a little label with "Bunnyboiler" on it, make up some scarves and sell them. For next winter, that's my knitting goal. Maybe I'll offer different designs, maybe I'll just experiment. It's not because I think I'll be good. It's just that I want to experience things. It's just trying new stuff. Even going and getting labels made professionally—I'll probably end up with

500 labels that I'll have to sew in my socks, but that's okay.' She leans in closer. 'It's like I've got this limited lifetime and I've always had this panic that I haven't got time to do everything that's out there . . . I just have to do this for me.'

What's more, doing all this is giving her a new appreciation for old skills. 'I look back at my grandmother—and I used to think, "It's just an old granny making a jumper,"—but now I see it's really a technical thing they do. There are a lot of mathematical calculations. I don't think we give them credit for what they're doing. There's technique—combining stitches, even deciding what size needles you need—and there's skill. I respect that a lot.'

There's a tide coming in and it's throwing up skills and ideas we almost lost.

Aoife Clifford, 30, is a union organiser in Melbourne with the National Union of Workers, which means she covers everything from poultry to manufacturing to call centres. A proud feminist with a legal background, Aiofe is the first point of call if there's a problem for her members. Again, she doesn't exactly fit the knitting granny stereotype.

Aoife was taught to knit by her mother when she was a child and she picked up sticks again eight years ago when she was sharing a house with another knitter. At first it was a practical thing to do, she says, living in cold-climate Canberra at the time, but more importantly it provided a balance to work and a creative outlet. Ever since then, she says with a trace of bemusement, 'We've been waiting for the revival.'

'I used to get worried in the wool shops—they seemed to be staffed by people who looked like they were about to retire—but in the last few years that's changed. There is a resurgence in the home and cooking. I think it's a reaction to the fast pace and people who have "it all" are realising parts of it aren't satisfying.'

'Knitting's taught me patience,' she says. 'At the start I wouldn't do tension squares [a square knit to calculate size] and now I do because I want my knitting to be good. It's a whole different way to work. Rather than churn through and get on with it, knitting can sit there for years.'

Aiofe is three months' pregnant and feeling the weariness of the first trimester, so she hasn't been knitting as much as she'd like, lately. 'I'll really love being able to knit for my children. I've knitted a few baby things for people at work,' she says, 'and what surprised me is how few people have anything knitted for them. They get quite emotional.' Which is true. There is something absolutely touching about someone spending their time, not their money, making you something by hand.

In fact women often start knitting when they are having their first child, which is what got Lisa Ryan, former IT professional, now mother of Ella, four and Luke, two, on her knitty way. 'What started me?' she says. 'Going into a store in Mosman and seeing a baby outfit for $150, that's what.' She laughs. 'I thought, if I can make a patchwork quilt, surely I can learn to knit.' Looking around her airy room I see several quilts draped out over the lounge. 'I quilted that one in the front seat of the car,' she says following my gaze, 'all the way up to Queensland.'

Lisa lives in Balgowlah, a leafy suburb next to Manly in Sydney. It's 12.30 p.m.—nap time for Ella and Luke—so we can talk. Unpacking a carefully folded hand-knit babywear collection out of her living room cupboard Lisa says, 'It's terrible. I've given away all the old clothes, but I haven't been able to part with anything I knitted. It's a labour of love.'

She lays the collection out on the broad table. 'This is the first thing I made for my daughter,' she says holding up a tiny blue and white cardigan. 'I said to the secretary at work who knits, "Do you think I can do this?" and she gave me a hand. Suddenly a pattern started appearing and I'm going, "I'm doing it, I'm doing it."' Lisa gestures animatedly at the memory. 'Now,' she adds, 'even cables aren't so hard.'

Lisa gets out an A4 workbook and opens it up, revealing pages and pages of handwritten knitting notes. In learning to knit she's decided to apply the skills she used when she taught IT. 'I used to say to my students, "If you look at the whole manual it will just freak you out, so let's just look at it a page at a time. And if a page freaks you out, lets just look at one paragraph." I use this for knitting. Each time it gets easier and easier, you build up skills. I'm finally knitting my first adult jumper for me.'

Now she says, 'I need this to create some balance. It's definitely relaxing,' she adds, 'which I didn't realise when I started, especially after a stressful day of children.' She brings over her knitting encyclopedia. 'I lie in bed and flick through these at night,' she confesses, 'isn't that pathetic?'

'I really want to teach Ella to knit and sew,' says Lisa, 'I want her to try everything. Look,' she adds, 'I change the ending of *Snow White*. She goes off to uni and becomes an actress, but I don't think that by knitting she is going to be a wuss. It's part of tradition. I want the same for my son.'

Lisa's been thinking a lot about balance and staying home, having given up work reluctantly when Luke was one when it became clear that balancing motherhood and a profession at that stage in her children's life wasn't working. 'I earned good money, I was a manager, I had a great job and it was challenging,' she says. 'Unless I could get that again, I'd rather be knitting and taking my kids to the park.'

'I think women have been so busy proving we could do it,' she says thoughtfully, 'and we've had to work so hard to be seen as equal. Maybe we were so focused on the end goal that we missed things on the way. I didn't want kids until I was 30, then I did. What is important to me now is the things I tell my son and daughter. And just being a decent person, trying to live my life with integrity and decency and that goes back to tradition. This whole myth that you can have it all is just that, a myth. You can have it at different times in your life, but with kids your priorities change. Now the career thing, I've done it. I don't have to prove that to myself. And I really didn't want my kids to be raised by strangers.'

'The feminist thing became so judgemental,' she says. 'What we need is a range of choices for all women.'

I think of what Tiffany said earlier: 'The big factor, I suppose, is choice. I choose to cook most nights, knit clothes for the family, grow my own herbs. For many generations these were necessities and thus rather eagerly thrown off.' Knitting is part of having choices in your life. Choosing to have a career, a nice home, a family and other interests. What are these third-wave feminists if not the choice generation? That is where our freedom lies.

You don't have to look further than to the feminist grandmothers to find an eloquent articulation of that idea. Virginia Woolf famously argued '. . . It is necessary to have five hundred a year and a room with a lock on the door if you are to write fiction or poetry.' A room of one's own and an income. No arguments there. Yet, she also wrote to a friend asking, 'Does housekeeping interest you at all? I think it really ought to be just as good as writing, and I never see . . . where the separation between the two comes in. At least if you must put books on one side and life on the other, each is a poor and bloodless thing. But my theory is that they mix indistinguishably.' Maybe our feminist grandmothers were onto something too.

I wonder, did Virginia Woolf knit?

Knitting Diary, 11 June 2002
Decide to jump on bandwagon. Must be something to this. I am going to knit too. Survey friends about where to start. 'Tapestry Craft,' whispers Joanne conspiratorially. 'Tapestry Craft,' says Tiffany. 'Best in NSW'. 'They're having a sale,' says Danni. Think I'm onto something.

Tapestry Craft is the Sydney knitters' most cherished open secret. They advertise but you'll probably hear about it word-of-mouth. It's located in the heart of the city on York Street right next to the yuppy Forbes Hotel that is jammed most nights with smart suits and beers.

But right now it's 10.30 a.m. on Tuesday and the city has a mid-morning quiet, with only couriers and delivery men whizzing by. The tapestry section is below street level, while a sign in the window directs you upstairs to the third floor for wool. The lobby directory next to the lift shows the building also houses both Right to Life and War Veterans.

I press the button to the third floor. A couple of middle-aged women bustle in with me when the doors open. 'You come regularly?' one is asking. 'I make a day of it,' says the other.

The lift opens and I follow them left to the fluorescent-lit shop. It's a woolaphile's paradise. Piles of sealed packets of yarn lie flat on benches. Mohair, wool, acrylic, endless colours. Being June, everywhere red signs advertise sale time. People are grabbing bag-loads.

I notice scarves made with different stitches pinned up on the walls. 'Pink bobble things,' I note, 'blue bumpy ones.' I can't remember the proper terms.

Over the other side is a bookshelf filled with orphan balls.

Right in the middle I see it: a rich, red mohair, flecked with blue and yellow. There's only one. I quickly pounce.

The activity seems to revolve around a curly-haired woman—Linley Valente—who whirls through the store. 'I'll be right with you,' she tells an anxious pattern-waver. 'Yes, we have that colour,' she's announcing down the phone. 'There's plenty for that,' she says to someone at the counter.

I gently tug at an airy mohair scarf floating in front of me. 'That will make that,' says Linley whisking past, looking at my lone ball.

'Only one ball?' I ask.

'Just one ball,' she says. 'Size 10 needles, cast on 19 stitches, rib stitch.'

I nod blankly, 'Oh rib,' I say. 'Um, remind me.'

'You know,' she says, 'knit one, purl one and then reverse on the following row.'

'Of course,' I lie. 'What size needles did you say?'

'Come with me,' she says, taking me up the back of the shop. 'These are the best, Australian made, from cowsmilk,' she says of a milky plastic pair.

'I'm a beginner,' I finally say unhelpfully at the counter.

'You'll pick it up fast,' she says. 'That's why I put my scarves up, so you can see what you can do.'

I talk with the cashier, who, as it turns out, is Albert

Morris, manager of this section and son of the woman who started the company two decades past. The knitting section is a fairly recent addition, introduced only three years ago. 'Every second person wrote down "knitting" in the visitors book,' Albert says, 'that's the only reason we saw the trend coming.' From the day the wool arrived it's been walking out the shop.

But is it just this shop, in this one part of town?

'It started two seasons ago,' says Greta Gergely of Greta's Handcraft Centre in Lindfield, on Sydney's North Shore train line. 'Young Asian girls first, asking for wool. Then this year it just went though the roof. We had no supplies. I get sick in my stomach waiting for the next shipment to come in.'

Greta is a 25-year veteran of the trade. There used to be four specialty wool shops on the north side. Greta's is the last left standing. In the last big slump through the 1990s, knitters dropped off and the big craft shops carrying discount wool almost killed the rest. Greta says she only stayed because it's her hobby—she also knits costume pieces for the Australian Opera and movies. She doesn't make much money out of it. Still, she is glad to be around as the market turns again. Standing a short pace away a mother, daughter and granddaughter team are mid negotiations over wool for the grandmother to knit a baby outfit. 'Stronger colours,' the 30-something mum is saying, 'not those pastels.'

Knit or Myth #1

THE ORIGINS OF KNITTING

Knitting, depending on who you choose to believe, began with Eve, the ancient Egyptians, the Ancient Greeks, the Roman Egyptians, the Vikings or the Arabs.

The case for Eve as the inventor of knitting goes back to a supposed Yemeni story that has Eve in the Garden of Eden knitting the pattern on the serpent's back. As far as creation stories go, it's a good one, but as for reliable proof . . . ? This story is regrettably consigned to myth.

The case for the knitting Pharaohs comes from the claim by some Egyptologists that the long bone pins found in the tombs of the Pharaohs might have been knitting needles. This is apparently based solely on the fact that these crafty-minded scholars thought they look like knitting needles. Fabulous speculation, yes. Historical proof, sadly, no.

The Greeks get a guernsey thanks to Homer's *Odyssey*, where the story of undying love between Odysseus and Penelope is recounted. After failing to return from his long voyage Odysseus was feared dead. It was the Greek custom for the widow to remarry, but the ever-loving Penelope clung to her hope that Odysseus would come back. She began making a shroud, telling her unwelcome suitors that once it was finished she would choose from among them. However, each night the plucky Penelope secretly unravelled her day's work, buying herself time. As for the proof that it was knitting she was undoing? Her work is described as the same on both sides—like knitting—and presumably unravelling is easier for a knitter than a weaver. A most unlikely proof.

The first knitting fashion faux pas certainly belongs to the Roman Egyptians, who settled along the Nile around the second century AD. They made what are now confusingly called 'Coptic Socks'. These natty little numbers were knitted with the big toe separated from the rest of the sock to accommodate the thong of a sandal. Yes, these early knitters unforgiveably encouraged the wearing of socks and sandals. And to prove that all knitting fashions just go around, another pair of Coptic socks was found, sized for a child and coloured in garish bands of blue, red, violet, yellow and green. Grandma, it seems, has always delighted in humiliating the young ones. While undoubtedly knit fabric, these socks were unlikely to have been knitted with two needles as today, but with a rather more complicated 'nal binding' system, a technique that more closely resembles crochet, and in this case was done with an eyed needle.

That the Vikings knitted, raped and pillaged is a story that sounds too good to be true. And it is. But Viking garments—or at least the fragments which have been found—do show trimmings with a kind of knitted braid. But rather than being made by a pair of needles, they are most likely 'sprang', a form of finger knitting.

In fact, as far as true hand-knitting of the sort we do today goes, it's most likely this came to the west the same way Aristotle and the Greek myths did—from Islamic Egypt. Fustat, in what is now modern Cairo, was the capital for the newly conquered Islamic Egypt in the seventh century. Knitting samples have been recorded there from this time. Islamic Egypt also brought us the first socks-with-slogans centuries before Nike thought of it. Socks dating anywhere between 1200–1500 feature the name 'Allah' knitted in prominently, along with geometric trimming.

'I think the trend will keep going so long as they keep bringing in interesting yarns,' says Greta. 'The movie stars in America started it.'

Down in Melbourne, Sue Green is contemplating her new investment. A former journalist, then former woolshop employee, she has just bought Sunspun Inspirations, a long-established knit shop known for its high-end products. 'I only took over a month ago,' she says, 'it's a risk but knitting is having a big revival.'

Across town at the Southbank markets Sue Flynn is doing a roaring trade with her Hawthorne Cottage Yarns, wool that is home-grown and hand-spun from the Leicester sheep she farms in Ballarat, two hours' north in central Victoria. Some of the skeins she has flying colours in her display are still wet. She was cleaned out of supplies last week and had to hurriedly spin and dye another batch for today.

Over in Perth it's the same story. 'I was surprised how much this business took off,' says Emma Eaton of the Woolshack, a new Perth-based online wool shop. 'I think there's a shift in people's perceptions about what knitting's all about.'

Everywhere I turn, something is going on in the woolfields, something big. It's boom time. They're not keeping up with the demand now and it just keeps growing.

Knitting Diary. 11 June 2002

Home from Tapestry Craft. Hold set of cowsmilk needles in one hand, ball of wool in the other and make slipknot. What now? Ring Mum. 'I can't remember how to cast on,' I say. She laughs. A lot. 'Who'd have thought you'd ever be asking that?' she finally says. After a couple of failed attempts to describe the process she goes and gets her old knitting so she has it in front of her when she's describing it. We manage to cast on together. I cast on 18. It looks too narrow. I cast on another 4. Somehow remember how to knit and purl. I haven't done this for twenty years but it's a bit like riding a bike. You just remember.

Two hours later when Rob comes home am still knitting. 'Aren't you meant to be writing?' he asks suspiciously. 'Research,' I say triumphantly, holding up 10 cm of work. 'I'll just do one more row.'

CHAPTER TWO

Knitting is the new yoga

Q. *I was recently most alarmed to see two knitters swap needles. Quite openly, in daylight too. I felt this most foolhardy. Could you please advise, is it okay to share needles?*

A. As my dear father often said when refusing us an advance on our pocket money, 'never lend what you are not prepared to lose' and I think this useful principle applies to sharing needles. I have been approached by friends, generally novices, to loan them a needle. In most cases I refuse. For a start I think the borrowing of needles shows a lack of commitment to the craft. I will, however, make an exception if a friend, in dire circumstances, discovers that the cuffs of a certain cardigan require a different size needle to the rest. Like lending a cup of sugar, it would be churlish to refuse. Although, if possible it would be better to give them your second-best pair as you would be quite wrong to expect even a devoted knitter to take the same care with your needles as you do yourself. To set your mind at ease, there are no known health risks involved in the practice.

Knitting Diary. 11 July 2002

Wake up in excruciating pain. Can hardly move. Have trouble breathing and swallowing. Niggling neck pain yesterday has turned into body-cast stiffness today. Drive to osteopath to beg appointment. Do convincing hunchback impression at reception. 'I'll see anyone,' I say, 'anytime.'

Two hours later osteo Kate helpfully observes I'm very hunched in. 'Have you been doing anything unusual lately?' she asks.

'Not really,' I tell her, 'I've been writing a bit, and knitting.'

In truth last week was spent entirely hunched over a computer or hunched over my knitting. Had started Rob's jumper (20 ply wool, big needles). Work satisfyingly fast. Almost finished back. Kate keeps straight face. 'That would be it,' she says. After soothing massage she asks, 'You don't mind if I manipulate your neck do you?' So this is what knitting has come to. 'You might hear a pop,' she says. 'Pop' is bone crunching 'crack' that shudders through my body. Still, can now breathe again. Kate recommends further treatment and I'm sent away with instructions to hunch less. At home, drop another pink pain pill and reluctantly put knitting aside.

'I'm addicted to yarn. I just ordered $60 in yarn for myself,' states Keith Courville, perhaps the unlikeliest advocate for the benefits of knitting. Ever.

The *Denver Post* describes killer Keith Courville—his biceps covered with tattoos, including a depiction of the grim reaper—sitting in his cell at the maximum security Limon Correctional Facility in Colorado, USA, surrounded by dozens of multicoloured skeins of yarn. He's crocheting a beanie cap.

Courville is one of 90 prisoners at the facility who knit caps, teddy bears, dolls, scarves and mittens for homeless or poor children across Colorado. It's part of a therapy and rehabilitation program for some of the state's most dangerous criminals.

'This is my escape,' he says, 'You get off on this and you lose track of anything else. If you don't have something that focuses you in another direction, you get meaner.'

Truth be told the main goal of the nine-year-old program is managing problem criminals, keeping them quiet and out of trouble: a third of the offenders are serving life terms. Still, before his addiction to yarn, Courville was addicted to crystal methamphetamines and sold drugs on the street. In 1983, strung out on drugs, he shot a friend dead and then shot another person shortly after. 'I didn't care for me so I didn't care for anybody else,' he says. A few years ago he had an epiphany and realised staying on his current course would keep him locked up the rest of his life. He enrolled in a school diploma program and discovered a love of writing poetry and children's stories. Now he has been out of trouble for six years and is knitting on the straight and narrow.

Okay, so perhaps not every serial killer is going to be rehabilitated by knitting. On the other hand, growing evidence suggests that crafting has more than just a creative effect, it has a calming one as well. And if knitting can calm down a stressed-out, hardened criminal, surely it has its uses for the stressed-out career woman, particularly the serial overworker.

Knit one, purl one, knit one, purl one—there's something in the rhythm of that soft mantra that many women crave. 'I find it calming,' agrees Tiffany. 'It's something I need to do,' says Danni. 'It's meditation,' says Joanne, 'constructive meditation.' The 'm' word comes up in most knitting conversations.

Joanne Yates, 33, is a professional lobbyist, with years of experience striding the halls of power in Canberra and New South Wales. She's advised politicians, lobbied for the film industry and is now the Executive Officer for the New South Wales Police Commissioner. She's smart, funny and fearsome.

Joanne arrives in a neat dark suit and tidy heels at Pontoon, a popular bar at Sydney's Cockle Bay. As the late afternoon sun sets over the water, with cocktail in hand,

Joanne has a yarn about her knitting passion. She's been a knitter since she was fourteen. 'One of my biggest years of knitting was my HSC year,' she comments. 'I relax with it, indulge time, it is meditative.'

For Joanne the time-consuming aspect of knitting is a bonus. 'Time is an indulgence,' she says, of her own demanding career. 'My interpretation about my own feminism is it's about my own time,' she continues. 'It's about value, it can't just be about the economic.'

It's true. No matter what the rhetoric, most workplaces haven't really become more feminised than a generation ago. We're working longer hours, not less. We're doing bigger mortgages, harder deals and short-term job contracts.

Time is our commodity now. We hoard it, juggle it, and trade off pay for it. We're as time poor as money poor. So what could be more radical now than spending time? Knitting forces you to sit still. In our complicated juggling lives it is something so simple. Sit down. Pick up a needle. Pick up some wool. Knit a stitch. Knit another. Just be.

'The whole knitting experience is tactile,' says Joanne, 'the feel of the wool, the colour, the size of the ply.' Knitting is creative, earthy and fundamental. It softens the hard corporate edges we've had to develop.

In fact, according to research conducted by the Craft Yarn Council of America, the number one motivation for people to knit is to relax. Research reported from the Mind Body Institute at Harvard Medical School also found that knitting and embroidery were as effective as meditation, yoga or chanting in triggering the body's relaxation response. When you're knitting the repetitive motions block the hormone noradrenaline, which in turn lowers blood pressure causing you to feel peaceful. In one study, needleworkers' heart rates dropped by up to eleven beats a minute while they worked. It's not hard to see why it becomes addictive.

Sue Gordon Lydon is so convinced of the meditative power of knitting that she's written a whole book on it called *The Knitting Sutra*. In it Lydon details how she knitted her way out of drug addiction, which in turn sent her on a spiritual quest. The quest threatened to overwhelm her with the myriad of spiritual options that appeared. 'I needed knitting not only to save my mind from [twelve-step recovery] boredom, but also to find my way through the confusing thicket of spiritual options that now appeared to me,' she writes. 'It was a haven of peace I could retreat to whenever I became overwhelmed.'

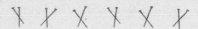

The purpose of meditation is to quieten the mind so that it can sink down into contemplation of its true nature. You cannot stop your mind by an act of will anymore than you can stop the beating of your own heart . . . I believe that in the quiet, repetitive, hypnotic rhythms of creating craft, the inner being may emerge in all its quiet beauty. The very rhythms of the knitting needles can become as incantatory as a drumbeat or a Gregorian chant.

I think of Marion East, a knitter in Canberra. Marion is an artist who lives out the back of a house in Lyneham in a tiny converted garage-studio crammed with bookshelves groaning Virginia Woolf; comfy chairs piled with hand-knit blankets; a proper sideboard with proper teacups; and her own vivid red-riot expressionist painting of a dog on the far wall.

'I've knitted through every life crisis,' she says. 'It saved my sanity when my marriage broke up.' With just her kids and living in a caravan, Marion says, 'I used to knit jumpers and just blubber. That rhythm and flow is important,' she says, 'it calmed me down. It was a focus, but also, when you're in the depths of despair it's a positive thing—you can make something beautiful and just concentrate on the object that's materialising in front of your eyes.'

Now also an art therapist, Marion hasn't been afraid to take this philosophy to extremes. On one of those early, particularly bad days, a grassfire near her house got out of control. While fire engines and firemen were tearing around the house Marion sat and knitted her cardigan. 'I just looked down and thought, the world can go to hell,' she says, conceding now that the whole scene was a tad Monty Python. Perhaps knitting can be a little too calming . . .

Someone else who swears by the therapeutic use of knitting is Kelley Deal. Kelley, along with identical twin sister Kim, are The Breeders, punk legends in alterna-rock circles. The Breeders were first formed by Kim a decade ago, and soon included Kelley in the line-up. After the first album great things were predicted, but the early 1990s were also the start of Kelley's dark days, when her longstanding addiction to heroin went from being a secret to being a problem. Arrest for possession in 1994 was followed by the beginnings of rehab in 1995. All of which would pack neatly into a stock standard rock 'n' roll bio if it weren't for the addiction Kelley picked up the following year—knitting.

Knit or Myth #2

THE KNITTING VIRGINS

Knitting as a craze hit Europe big in the Middle Ages. It was particularly popular for producing garments and homewares like cushions—and just check this year's knitting trend. Heraldic patterns were popular, as were eagles and lions. The fact that they mostly appeared in Spain—still under Moorish influence—reinforces the Muslim knitting heritage.

In keeping with its great tradition of appropriating all useful stories, the Catholic Church soon got in on the act. During the fourteenth century, paintings of the Madonna and child become more emotional and domestic and what better picture of hearth fire bliss is there than a woman knitting at home, infant by her side? Enter the knitting Madonnas. The most famous of these, the 'Madonna dell'umilita' (Madonna of humility—she's sitting on the floor) by the brothers Lorenzetti finds Mary knitting in the round with four needles and purple yarn, a dozen or so bobbins nearby. What this tells us about everyday knitting is a moot point: it may or may not indicate that knitting was a common activity: maybe it was only done by the nobility (purple thread) or perhaps only by the common woman (on the floor). A couple of centuries later the church was also to claim crochet, which is still referred to as 'nun's work' in some parts of the world.

Still, those making a case for knitting as a virtue certainly would have approved of the English at this time. In 1571 The Cappers Act stipulated that on Sundays and Holy Days everyone above the age of six years had to wear a knitted cap made by an English capper, making knitting one of the great protected industries of the time. Ladies and gentlemen, knights, travellers, lords and the rich were exempt, naturally.

'Once I start talking about knitting you won't shut me up,' warns Kelley cheerily down the phone from her homebase in Dayton, Ohio, USA. 'First I've got to tell you something cool that happened in Europe. We had a Dutch documentary crew do a one-hour special on The Breeders. In the film there was a lot of me knitting—it looked really cute—and they showed this a lot in Holland and Belgium. Then we did the big summer festivals over there and my fans bombarded me with yarn on stage.' She continues with bemused delight: 'They were so considerate—it was rainy and muddy and they'd carefully packaged it in plastic bags. I got 15–20 skeins of wool and some of it is really old and really exotic. A lot of other band members—The Black Rebel Motor Cycle Club, Filter, really heavy stuff—were looking at me going, "What are your fans throwing?"'

The knitting started when Kelley was touring with her band, the Kelley Deal 6000. 'When you're touring you have a lot of time travelling,' she explains, 'and it used to be drugs and alcohol that took that time. Then I got sober and I needed something to do.' She discovered that Katrine, the girlfriend of the drummer from their support band the Radar Brothers, was a knitter. The next stopover they jumped off and Kelley bought a sweater pattern, needles and wool and Katrine taught her how to knit. 'The sweater is completely unwearable,' she laughs. 'Now when people are learning to knit I say, "Start with a scarf."'

Now sober, Kelley has most definitely swapped one set of needles for another and her new addiction is running rampant. 'On the last tour I had one suitcase full of clothes and two suitcases of knitting yarn, crochet needles, beads, thread and all kinds of strange handles,' she says. 'On tour I knit every day and when I get off tour I have a knitting room. I'm sitting in it right now.'

In fact, Kelley has parlayed her knitting compulsion into a handy business, knitting and felting handbags that she sells online <www.kelleydeal.net> and through a trendy shop on Sunset Boulevard in Los Angeles. 'It's not a choice now,' she says, 'I'm definitely addicted. If I didn't sell them I'd have a room full. I'd have a 1000 a year.'

Ever the creative, Kelley never follows patterns so every purse is one of a kind. She's found ways to incorporate her music into her bags too, by including musical hardware like guitar strings and drum keys in the pattern. And she's cunningly crafted a way to turn her non-knitting sister Kim into her beading slave. 'What will happen,' she giggles, 'we'll be sitting there in our apartment in LA and I'll be knitting, and I'll think, I need a beaded strap for this bag. So I'll get it all organised: get out the beads, pick the colours, and just lay it out on a saucer. Kim's a smoker, so she'll pick up a big old joint, and before you know it she picks up the beads, plays with them and after an hour—she's very Zen—she'll have done the beading. So I've got my very own slave person.'

And while not it's not knitting, Kelley has also found a way of incorporating one of her crafts into her music. Also a quilter, she has rigged up her sewing machine—zigzag stitch is best—for the rhythm track on more than one album. 'I was doing a Willie Nelson tribute album, called *Twisted Willie*, and I did a song with Kris Kristofferson, "Angel Flying Too Close to the Ground",' she recounts. 'We wanted the rhythm track to be really haunting and scary. So here's Kris Kristofferson with his headphones on telling the guy, "I need a little less guitar and a little more sewing machine."'

A knitting room of one's own, 1000 knitted bags a year and a solid punk career. Maybe not quite what Virginia Woolf had in mind, but she probably would have approved.

Knitting Diary. 17 July 2002

Have second osteopath appointment to fix neck. 'How is the writing going?' asks osteo Kate innocently, waiting until am lying face down immobilised before adding, 'How's the knitting?' Suspect she finds it funny. 'I've put it down for a few days,' I tell her. Kate pokes painful gap between shoulder blades and spine and tells me I'm still tight. This is not news. Have to be bone-crunched again. Feel pathetic and ridiculous. Knitting-related impairment adds insult to injury. Could accept injuring back running the bulls in Pamplona or from hurling myself out of a plane. Still, at the end of the session feel terrific.

Can move neck again. Shoulders don't ache. Decide to take celebratory knit trip to Champion Textiles, two blocks up road.

It is a clear late winter Friday afternoon and the first whispers of spring are warming the air. There's a happy chatter coming from St Joseph's community hall in Rozelle, Sydney, even though it is pitched right on the edge of Victoria Road, one of the busiest roads into town. This is where one of the city's most popular knitting classes takes place—led by the redoubtable Liz Gemmell. Sitting behind desks arranged in a big U shape around the room are pairs and threes of women knitting, who range in age from mid-thirties to retirement.

Susannah, 36 years old, has been coming for a year now. A former high-flyer, she has worked in advertising, theatre management and finance. Then three years ago she had a wake-up call that well, eventually triggered knitting.

'I was a bit of a career person,' says Susannah, words laced with a Lancashire accent tumbling fast out of her mouth. 'I worked 90 hours a week, had a really active social life, lots of going to the gym.' Then she got chronic fatigue syndrome. With the helpless shrug of someone long resigned she adds,

'I basically spent a year in bed. I was weak as a kitten. There was literally nothing I could do. You have a complete body breakdown. I couldn't read anymore, not even trashy novels. I couldn't watch TV either. I just couldn't even follow a soapy plot.'

Not a great space to be in for someone who had been so driven and active. But it was when her mother came out from England to look after her that Susannah got the idea. 'My mum was knitting and she said "You have to do something—maybe you could knit."' For the first time in months, she had something she could do. 'At first I could only do little bits,' she recounts, ' I worked my way up from ten minutes to half an hour.' It was just simple knitting. Susannah could concentrate long enough to make one stitch, then another, and then put it down when it got too tiring. She knitted one square—a sample—10 cm x 10 cm. Then another, and another, 'I just kept knitting those,' she says, ' then a baby's jumper, a baby's blanket. Then four jumpers for Jonathan.' Jonathan, who has come to pick her up from class, smiles shyly.

'Knitting made me want to get up,' she says, 'I'd been housebound and I practically got anxiety attacks if I went to a shopping centre.' She called the community college who encouraged her join up and have made sure she can keep coming even if her funds run low.

Now mostly recovered, Susannah says with satisfaction, 'I feel I've created something. The better I get, the healthier I get, the more complicated the knitting gets.' Nowadays, when her mother comes out from the UK, she comes along to the classes as well. 'It's a great family atmosphere here, it's a little fellowship. It keeps me sane. It's kind of like AA,' she says smiling, 'everyone helps everyone else.'

I look around the room again. A university lecturer is chatting with a retired fencing instructor. Housewives chat to a young mum. It's got an old-fashioned, neighbourly, chat-over-the-back fence atmosphere. 'Now,' says Susannah with the broad grin of a woman on a mission, 'I'm trying to reclaim the right to knit wherever I want. I knit in every room of the house. I knit on buses. Anywhere.'

Knitting Diary, 17 July 2002

Walk to Champion Textiles straight after osteo. Champion is off the side of boho-slacker King Street, Newtown, Sydney, so you won't stumble across it on a lazy ramble down the strip. First heard about it on knitters' grapevine, and it has a wonderful lost-in-time haberdashery air, slotted into old warehouse building. Unchanged for generations. The real deal. A true, old-

fashioned wool and crafts shop. 'You're back,' says Gloria, recognising me as I'm chimed in the door.

'I need some wool,' I say, 'beige and maroon. Four ply. Knitting a scarf for Dad.'

'We'll find something,' says Gloria waving me down the back to the 4 ply row, 'we're running our stocks low as we're about to upgrade to a position on King Street.' Of course.

CHAPTER THREE

The
good
life

Q. *My sister and I are not speaking. She maintains that knitting is about a return to nature and that only pure wool is acceptable. I maintain practicality must play a part. Synthetics are washable, and anyway, lurex really jazzes up a bedjacket. I am wondering if you could answer me, natural or synthetic?*

A. Ah yes, I well remember an early humiliation at the Knitter's Guild when I pulled out what I still regard as a particularly stylish and fashionable beret knitted with metallic and synthetic yarn. The laughter and opprobrium is still ringing in my ears. In my feeble need to fit in I quickly learnt my lesson: 'It's natural or nothing'. As a consequence I didn't experiment at all with anything that wasn't 100 per cent natural for years. I regret this now. Synthetic drugs also have much to offer us. Who needs elk horn when you have Viagra? Life is too short. If it feels good, do it.

Knitting Diary. 23 July 2002

*Into the abyss. Have just come from Greta's Handcraft
Centre in Lindfield, THE wool shop of Sydney's North
Shore. Have not finished single item of knitting yet and
now have two more projects. So excited about 100-ply
thick honey beige and grey wool that I cast on scarf in
car before next appointment. Is daytime knitting a bad
sign? The sun was just past the yardarm.*

While most knitters happily rely on a regular hit of click-clack
stress relief to get them through their day, there is another
group that takes this much further. Once these knitters take
up the needles there is no point of return. They're on a quest.
They're not just managing their lives, they're changing them.

For Eva Gerencer, 34, a migrant community worker and
web designer, knitting is part of a complete life change.
It started when she turned 30 and left the city, moving to the
Blue Mountains west of Sydney. With the move away also
came a return to study, a change to eating organic vegetables
and moving in with her partner. Cook, belly dancer, dance
teacher, gardener, renovator and knitter, with some classes in

aromatherapy and soap making as well, Eva is making over her life.

'Why did I start knitting?' she says with a quick laugh. 'I moved to a cold climate.'

But, she continues, 'Really it was to have the satisfaction of creating something myself, rather than just buying a mass-produced product.' Eva is looking for something more than a job and something more than just what money can buy. 'It's a very practical thing,' she says, 'and it's interesting to keep an old craft going. What was really interesting was who I learnt it from.'

Last year a few of the staff members where Eva worked were interested in learning to knit. Being community workers—Eva works with recently arrived African refugees—they looked to their community for expertise.

'There was a Sudanese woman—Mary,' says Eva, '80 years old, and she had a degree in costuming and dressmaking from Egypt. She had a photograph album of amazing pictures of bridal outfits and embroidery she'd made.' They had found their teacher. Eight women: five staff, the rest newly arrived migrants. After the first run of classes finished Eva kept going, taking private classes at Mary's modest townhouse.

'I want to have more simplicity in my life,' she says, 'Connect to the way things are created. In aromatherapy there is more satisfaction in using oils you have mixed yourself. It is good to know you don't always have to rely on the pre-packaged stuff. We grow our own vegetables now and it's the same thing. When you're working and you're in the city, you aren't connected to things. It is very satisfying to see something you've planted grow, something you've been knitting, made.'

She points out it isn't necessarily the cheaper option: 'To knit a good mohair will cost you $60 in materials, but I don't look at it that way. I think a lot of it is that satisfaction of creativity, but also practical. I like having a finished product.'

It's an approach not too many steps removed from *The Good Life*, the old 1970s British comedy about a couple trying to live self-sufficiently in the suburbs. But there is a more serious idea behind it. There is this notion that in a modern industrial economy like Australia, very few of us ever get to conceive, execute and complete a job. Instead we're all working in a sausage factory, where we're all just producing bits of meat for the sausage that somebody else stuffs. Because no-one sees a job through from beginning to end, no-one ever gets to feel a sense of completion—or satisfaction—with their work. Maybe knitting is one of the few things we actually get to do from start to finish.

Knit or Myth # 3

GOOD QUEEN BESS AND THE KNITTING MACHINE

Those enamoured with the hand-crafted aspect to knitting owe a debt of gratitude to Queen Elizabeth I, an early knitting enthusiast. Not that she was actually known to knit herself, but she was a champion of the new knitted silk stocking. Indeed her desires became so quickly known that by 1561 she received at least three pairs of silk knitted hose, imported from Spain, as gifts from commoners. In her court, the man leading the charge to miniskirts for men (which necessitated stockings to keep the legs elegant) was her favourite dandy—Robert Dudley, Earl of Leicester. Robert is on the record objecting to a shortage of supply. Shortly thereafter we also have the first recorded lament about laddering, Ben Johnson beginning his 1614 play *Bartholomew Fair* with a stagekeeper complaining that the lead actor would be out as soon as his stockings were stitched.

However, it is Elizabeth's role stymying the first knitting

machine for which she is notorious in knitting circles. This machine was invented by Nottingham gent William Lee in 1589, the year after the Spanish Armada sailed. There are two legends as to why he created the device and both involve revenge. The first has a besotted William pursuing a young woman who ran a successful knitting school. So successful in fact, that she had no time for any other interests, including William. The scorned William set about exacting his revenge by inventing a machine that could put her out of business. The second legend has William courting a young woman who did not put aside her knitting when he visited her, something he felt was a slight. To repay her coldness he set himself to making a machine that would render redundant her consuming passion for knitting. Whatever the real reason—and let's not discount good old-fashioned entrepreneurship here—William experimented with a frame for nine years, exhibited it and then applied to Queen Elizabeth I for a patent. Kind historians recount that she refused to offer a patent because she feared it would deprive her hand-knitting subjects of an income. Unkind ones suggest that so devoted was Elizabeth to her silk stockings that she was disappointed with the rough woollen stockings the device produced. Whatever the reason, William was to die a pauper in France in 1610, his vision of machine knitting unrealised.

When it comes to a total change to the good life it's hard to beat Amanda Ducker. Amanda, 34, is a former Paris correspondent for *Elle* magazine, former Features Editor of *Vogue*, and now knitwear designer with her own label, Minx Handknits. She lives in Nundle in New South Wales, an hour from country music capital Tamworth. 'I used to take my knitting to the pub and sometimes there was a feeling that I didn't belong,' she says of her old days living in Eastern Suburbs Sydney. 'I kept the knitting, but dropped the crowd.' Now in Nundle, she jokes, 'A lot of men will do anything for me for a jumper.'

Until recently, Nundle was just another slowly dying country village. Then Judy Howarth came to town. Judy and husband Peter have progressively bought up buildings in town, renovated them and leased them out, creating the award-winning Jenkins Street guesthouse and Cha! Cha! Cha! restaurant. It's a good story and ever the journalist, Amanda sniffed it out and came to town to write it up. A few months later she was back with all her things in tow.

'I just think there's a level of dissatisfaction with the spectator lifestyle,' she tells me, down the phone. 'I s'pose it's mostly the younger generation, the natural home-made thing is symbolic for people who are interested in the environment. The real thing is happening in Nundle. I knit with my friends down by the river. Every time I see my friend Treva's husband, he's wearing a new hat she's knitted. If I need a calm day— and I need a lot of those days—Treva and I go walking in the bush, take our knitting and are so revived.'

Knitting home-knit hats by a lazy river. That settles it. I'm taking my needles and ball and going.

Nundle is a long and pretty five-hour drive from Sydney. By late afternoon when we finally turn off the main highway and towards the small town the sun is low and the land is coloured dirty gold with drought. For a town with a wool industry, there is an awful lot of beef cattle around. I see no sheep until 15 kilometres before the town, when suddenly around a corner there is a small flock.

Nundle is instantly charming. It's a one-of-everything kind of place: one school, one pub, one general store and one public swimming pool. You can walk its four streets in a pleasant ten-minute stroll, which takes you past the one retirement home, which on cue, has a lady knitting in the window in the gathering dark.

First off the next morning is a meeting with Judy Howarth, who is, with husband Peter, the owner of Nundle Woollen Mill. Out front are picnic tables and cheery flags waving. Inside the mill shop stocks woollen goods—both local and imported—with a considerable sprinkling of stockpile socks, created from the last wool glut that was finally sold off last year. Inside are Amanda's Minx designs—whimsical hippy chic for children and adults—as well as other designs for bolder 20 ply vests and cardigans. Already wool pilgrims are batting down the door. Today they are mostly retired people (it's a big stop for some of the tour buses that cater to that market, I later find out) but the mill is used to hosting everyone from primary school up.

Judy strides in with keen energy and dives behind the counter to pick up the incessantly ringing phone. She's wearing the mill shop's merchandise: a black wool polo and a cream thick cardie-vest. She has the restless air of someone used to juggling projects but when she speaks she looks you straight in the eye with her full concentration. You can see how she gets things done. Just back from a flying visit to Sydney she says straight up, 'You'll love this. I was with my son yesterday down at Bondi watching the Rugby, and three of the young women with us pulled out their knitting.'

Judy lives on a big cattle property 5 kilometres out of town. She and Peter first arrived ten years ago and cattle are still their main game. They're both from Sydney, though Peter's always had interests in the land. When they got here, 'The town was all barred up,' she says, 'everything was for sale.' So Peter and Judy set about turning the place around, buying up most of the buildings in town and progressively restoring them. First the guesthouse and restaurant, then the town store, a craft gallery, another hotel. After that, says Judy, 'We decided we had given people a reason to come, now they needed something to keep them overnight.' Enter the wool mill.

Now running for two years, the wool mill operates with a set of antique machinery bought and restored for the purpose. A catwalk runs above the factory floor, so soon Judy is ushering me through the shop and out the door onto the walkway. Handy cards explain each of the processes below. Down the far end wool bales spill open and the wool is progressively combed straight and rolled on large rollers, then spun through to the bright 8, 12 and 20 ply wool that is the mill's stock in trade. Over the other side the dyer's vats are steaming, while on a line outside thick cerise whirls wave to dry. 'We're trialling blackberry at the moment,' says Judy of next season's colours, 'it's such a pest here, it would be great to put it to use.'

Business is, to say the least, booming. 'Yesterday I had my first day off in over a month,' she says. 'Last week the phone rang every three minutes and we had to have two people just answering calls.' The reason is just one article in the *Women's Weekly*. It profiled Judy, Amanda and the town and gave out a pattern, with a number to call to order a wool pack. Around 500 calls later: 'We're struggling to keep up,' says Judy. 'We're two weeks behind in our orders. I've had to put on extra people.'

That kind of demand makes you wonder why magazines stopped running knitting patterns and department stores closed their haberdasheries. Judy, drawing heavily on her retail background in the rag trade, has some ideas on this. 'When we were doing our research,' she says, 'the reason that the mills had been closing in Australia is they simply haven't kept up with fashion. You only have to go to the Easter show,' she chuckles, 'and see the knitting there—but god love the old ladies who do it.' It's true. Knitting suffers from a fairly high dag quotient. 'With anything in the rag trade, at the end of the day, it's quality that will survive,' she says. Now the mill gets involved with students of textile and design—'We give them wool to see what they come back with'—and they give out a prize at a wool fashion parade.

'It's all a matter of how much energy you've got,' she says. 'It's a commitment.' While she says, 'Life's been good to us,' she is careful to point out that making it work 'has been a community effort'. Nowadays the community is pretty much behind them. A lot of the suspicion of the Sydney blow-ins evaporated as people started to get work from their ventures. 'One of the main reasons for the mill was to sustain the village,' she points out. The mill has been good for local employment—in addition to its operators there are now 26 knitters.

And Judy believes they're on top of a general trend in all their operations. 'We're into organic beef and I put wool in with that. The young mums don't mind hand-washing. The whole thing is back to nature, no chemicals and hand-knits. And the fact is, we can make wool into some really funky items.'

<hr>

The next morning I find out Amanda and daughter Zia have been laid low with the flu. In their photo in the *Women's Weekly*, Amanda and Zia smile out at the camera blonde and strong, both wearing multi-striped Minx designs. Today, suffering still, Amanda is more a fragile canary, tip-toeing into her sunlit brick courtyard to a seat. Underfoot the winter herbs straggle across borders that reach the mountain-framing hedge out front. Zia, her hair a pixyish halo of white gold, putters behind in her sandpit.

Her face turned up to the sun, Amanda talks about why she moved here two years ago. 'I just wanted to be away from it all,' she says, 'it seemed like a peaceful place. My reality here is so much about friendships and secret places. I don't think I've got to the bottom of what moving here was about. Having my daughter was definitely a big part. I love Sydney— it's my city—but I didn't belong in the culture anymore.'

Still a freelance journalist, she's sanguine about leaving behind the AbFab magazine lifestyle. 'I've never seen myself as a career woman, even though I have been,' she says, 'I never thought that career is enough. I've always been on a search for meaning. A lot of women where I was working were having babies and they'd be back after twelve months maternity leave in fear of losing their prized *Vogue* job. Betsy Brennan there was inspirational. She said "Go off and have your family. Your job will still be there in 25 years if you want it." She'd done that.

'Moving here was reclaiming my own life. My own sense of freedom. I didn't have a plan when I came here, I just thought I'd see how we went.'

Amanda started knitting for Zia, then when her grandmother died she inherited her wool collection. 'I made Zia a little jacket out of Ruthie's old wool,' she recounts. 'There was a real shift in the generations, a sad time. Then I kept knitting. I think I just got hooked again. It's that simple, it's an addiction. It feels like something that is mine that I've carried through for such a long time.'

'The idea for Minx just came to me. I call it funky family knitwear. I love doing things for the whole family. I like the idea of creating a garment that can be—without sounding too ridiculous—worn by a baby or a man. I just like playing with the colours, creating a sense of joy, of trying to see a family in my things. It's a vision, an idea, an inspiration.' At the same time, her fashion background can't be helped. 'I'm so aware of the dag factor,' she chuckles, 'I just felt I had to start from scratch. I have literally thousands of patterns from vintage pattern books.'

She pauses thoughtfully, looking around the garden, 'One of the things I've been thinking about while I've been sick is how important it is, when you go off somewhere, not to recreate the same busy-ness. I try not to use my phone number as a contact—it's all email. It's obviously not a good business strategy, but if I had that phone ringing all the time, it would destroy the peace. I still take it off the hook when I need to.'

Amanda even sees knitting bringing her full circle back to her first craft: 'I actually think all the knitting is going to improve my writing. I can get disheartened working on the longer pieces of fiction, but if I learn to treat them like a jumper—knit a little, put the time in each day and fiddle, I think I would get it right.'

So maybe the theory is right. We want to do things properly. We want to be useful. And creative. Find a place where we control our world. It's the Good Life with a twenty-first century twist.

Knitting Diary. 28 July 2002

Somehow acquired more wool. Thick 20 ply cerise Nundle wool. Gorgeous colour. And new cardigan pattern. Use large needles to be sure will be able to finish another project. Running out of places to stash wool. Go and buy special wool bin when cat discovers stash behind sofa and ruins expensive mohair. Cat permitted to live this time.

CHAPTER FOUR

The knitting circles

Q. *I recently found myself in a bind on a Saturday night. I had been invited to a party, but the scarf I was knitting was not quite finished. I politely rang up and told them I had to finish the project. Now they are not speaking to me. Was I wrong?*

A. Dear knitter, I'm afraid you have erred here, but only in your research. Clearly your fellow partyers are not knitters. To non-knitting ears, 'I have to finish my knitting' sounds like 'I have to wash my hair', an insulting non-excuse. Knitters are different. They understand. In fact, they'd probably say, 'Oh, bring it along, the more the merrier,' and you can find yourself set up in a most pleasant Saturday night knitting circle. When dealing with non-knitters, your excuses must involve infectious illness you couldn't possibly pass on to the host, or an ailing grandparent.

Knitting Diary. 23 July 2002 (evening)
Have decided to knit my friend Alistair a scarf for his fortieth birthday. But crisis. It is only three weeks away and have party to go to to watch final episodes of Buffy for the season. Plan to take to party as watching television anyway. Rob scandalised. Thinks this is rude and says will not defend me. Fortunately knitting rolls up in my handbag. Will decide at party.

Knitting may be calming and meditative but there's something about the clickety-clack of the needles that is darn chatty too, and pretty soon new knitters are looking to move from being solo to team players. Like bunnyboiler, Lisa Herrod, who has started to stitch herself up a knitting circle.

It started with just with one: 'Suzanne, my next door neighbour and I knit together quite often,' she says. 'I'll go and knock on her door and say "Feel like a knit?" and we'll pour a glass of wine and might watch telly.' Harmless enough, but Lisa confesses, 'Then I got the girls together,' adding, with missionary zeal, 'If I learn something, I have an obligation to share with other people.' It was a community-minded spirit not entirely appreciated at first.

Knit or Myth #4

OFF WITH THEIR HEADS

Few stories are enjoyed more by the modern knitter than that of the indefatigable Madame Defarge who knitted merrily away at the foot of the guillotine during the French Revolution as the heads rolled around her. Unfortunately for those obsessed by historical accuracy while there are accounts of the rent-a-crowd tricoteuses (knitters) of Robespierre—a detachment of mercenaries paid by the commune to insult the victims and generally greet their deaths—and they are often pictured knitting stockings, there is alas, no mention of a Madame Defarge. We can thank Charles Dickens for her invention in his *A Tale of Two Cities*.

Still, the time of French Revolution also produced the first knitting saint. Seven-year-old Jean-Baptise Marie Vianney and his little sister Marguerite were child shepherds from Dardilly, just north-west of Lyon, France. As was the custom of the time, when the two went out every day to graze the family donkey, cows and sheep they took their

knitting with them. Jean-Marie also carried a statuette of
the Madonna in his shirt and would make a shrine for it
with leaves and flowers in a hollow tree trunk, telling
Marguerite: 'Knit my stocking. I must go and pray down
there by the brook.' Unaccountably it is Jean-Baptise—the
Cure d'Ars—not Marguerite, who is the saint.

'We fell about laughing,' says Jo Paul, 32, a cheery, bossy
redhead, of Lisa's initial attempt at conversion. Still, two
weeks later Lisa, Jo (commissioning editor), Suzanne (interior
designer), Marie (publishing rights associate) and Nic (IT
systems administrator) were all in Lisa's retro-filled 1940s
apartment in Sydney's Bellevue Hill, learning to knit. 'It started
as really a good excuse for getting together,' says Jo of the
close-knit group. 'We're trying to get together once a week—
usually Thursday nights because we're so busy.'

To date the group has produced five scarves, three knit
pictures, and one free-form jumper. Jo confesses: 'I recently
caught myself on Sunday arvo watching *National Velvet* on
the TV while I was knitting, a cup of tea by my side.' Not
exactly the image she is used to projecting. ' Very grandma,'
she laughs, 'except we've decided there's a lot more swearing.'

But like clubs everywhere, it's taken a little while to sort out the ground rules. First cab off the rank, thou shalt not covet thy neighbour's progress: 'We're all used to being good at what we do,' says Jo. 'That first time Lisa had this really difficult wool for me to use and I was having trouble with it. She suggested I switch to something easier, and I was like, "No, I can make this." Never stand between a modern woman and her multi-skilling. Marie also confesses to knitting rage that first night. 'I just sat there sooking,' she says of her first all-thumbs attempts.

Second, you are only as strong as your weakest link. The group all started out on scarves but when Marie finished hers she didn't know how to cast off so she had to wait a frustrating week until she caught up with Lisa.

And while they're not quite sharing needles yet, there is a growing problem of addiction. Nic was busted one Saturday night late for a party. 'I rang her,' says Jo, 'and she said "I'm still at home, I've been knitting."' Jo herself swears she has her own knitting in check, but her non-knitting friends have had concerns it is out of control: 'My friends were having a cricket match and I asked if I could bring my knitting to the match,' she admits, 'I thought it would be fine but they were, "No, put it down . . . "' The rest of the knitting group were very sympathetic about that one, but that's the problem with co-dependent addicts isn't it? They reinforce each other.

On the plus side, Jo observes her knitting addiction has helped her replace some other ones. 'It's great for giving up smoking and for losing weight,' she says. 'You can't knit and snack at the same time.'

But it isn't just Lisa, Jo, Marie, Suzanne and Nicola who are in a girl club mood. All across the city girls are taking a decided turn for the Nanna and knitting up playgroups with their friends.

Take Sophie Lee for instance. The actress famous for hosting a cartoon show, starring in *Muriel's Wedding* and now a serious Sydney Theatre Company thespian, knits. And she does it in polite company too. 'The main reason I took it up is I wanted to have a club,' she confesses. In fact she's so keen on her club that the day after I call her agent to request an interview, Sophie herself phones back to make a time.

We're meeting for lunch in the healthy-smelling Macro wholefoods at Bondi Junction, a good food Mecca in Sydney's Eastern Suburbs. Macro sports isles of organic grains and produce. To the side, the constant whirr of health-blends being whizzed announces the always-crowded café. Sophie herself is the picture of health with clear pale skin and clear pale blue eyes, her hair scraped back. Dressed ahead of the trend in a 1980s-style T, with a wide leather strap around her wrist, she more than once gives a deflated 'oh, it's so nerdy' sigh, and looks a little sheepish. Still, she does have a style icon before her justifying the habit. 'When I heard Kate Moss was knitting, or maybe it was embroidering,' she says with a wry smile, 'it certainly made the idea palatable. If it's good enough for Kate Moss, it's good enough for me.' A new knitter, she is still working on her first scarf—'chocolate brown, green, denim-blue, cream all mismatched'—a process which is being sped along by some backstage knitting between matinee and evening performances of the play she is currently appearing in.

'So why did you begin knitting?' I ask.

She pauses. 'Before my wedding, my best friend and I were in LA—she was my bridesmaid—and we went to this craft shop,' she begins, 'we bought lots of pink rope and little beads with letters, Stars of David, and hearts, our initials, and we made these things for my wedding that had bells that rang when you shook them. Doing that was so much fun—much more fun than going out and drinking martinis. Once I got settled back in Sydney I thought, my girlfriends are important to me, and I wanted a way to catch up with them that wasn't just sitting in a pub drinking. Knitting meant there was another purpose and at the end of it you were making something you could wear, while at the same time eating, having a glass of wine, catching up on what's been happening to them in their world. There's only three of us,' she admits bemusedly, 'we're recruiting new members.'

'It was also an LA inspired thing,' adds Sophie. 'People are really into craft over there. There's lots of craft shops and people are in pottery clubs, perhaps because it's a sober, bonding activity you can do in your spare time without harming anyone. Contrary to popular belief,' she says, raising her eyebrows for emphasis, 'getting wasted is not acceptable over there. It's frowned upon. People must do it behind closed doors. Things like AA are really big. So if you want to do something fun with you friends you'll do things like go to Beverly Hot Springs and get cucumber rubs, or go to Whole-food Daily, which has the best macrobiotic food, and you have your wheatgrass shots together, instead of a tequila shot. I think it's that kind of mindset which is more attuned to doing things with other people that doesn't involve alcohol.'

'But why knitting?' I ask, 'why not a book club, or another craft?'

'Well, I would like it to be a book club,' she says, ' I would like it to branch out so that as we knit maybe we introduce a book. But it's fun, and it's not meant to be too serious, and not competitive either, which is a relief. Because my career is really competitive, I felt a real need to do something, be enthusiastic about and get stuck into something that isn't about "Are you the best?" "Where is this going to take you?" Nowhere, hopefully,' she says, answering her own question. 'In the way that men meet up with their friends every night in the pub. It has that sort of feel to it except that it's a more meaningful experience. We've all got something in common, we've all got knitting. I don't want it to get too complicated. I go to the gym in the morning and knitting club every second Thursday night, its just part of my schedule.'

'We even went away for a knitting retreat,' she adds of a recent weekend away at a beach house. 'We'd walk on a beach, then we'd do a two-hour knitting stint, then we had all these ambitious recipes that we cooked from, and it was just girls, and we played Trivial Pursuit and it sounds so nerdy but it was really fun.'

Sophie is revelling in the all-together girliness of it all. 'I love to have a strong network of women who'll be there to support you when the going gets tough,' she continues, 'which it invariably does at some point in your life. It's just another way—I don't know—of putting women together so that they can discuss issues. Like a support group, in a fun way.' She points out that she's been used to having control for a long time: 'I was a competitive teenager; unless I had a natural aptitude for something straight off, I wouldn't persevere if I was going to be second best, which is kind of typical of our generation. English class I loved because I was good at it; sport, I wasn't good at, so I didn't care about it.' Now in her thirties and married, she is starting to think differently, also studying Judaism two nights a week with a view to conversion. 'When you're an old lady, will you be satisfied if you put everything on hold for a career, or not even a career, for the promise of a job?' she asks. ' You make a decision to put more emphasis on other things, your marriage, having children, a knitting club, just being there for your friends when they need you. Not just everything being about you. It's not about being the best, or making the best scarf, it's really the mediative quality, the community aspect, the satisfaction of creating something.'

Knitting Diary. 24 July (later evening)
Party group more sympathetic to public knitting than husband. Said party knitting was not an insult to their conversation. Scarf progress slow, however. Working on skinny 4.5 needles with only 6 ply wool is a shock, especially knitting beastly slow moss stitch. Am now knitting compulsively during the day, as knitting provides excellent reason to avoid actual writing. Have to ration myself to one row only between work phone calls. Knit one, call one, knit one, call one.

CATERING THE KNIT-IN

One of the imponderables: knitting is mediative, slow, yet we yearn to do it socially. It engages our hands, yet we yearn to eat while doing it. Thus catering is one of the great challenges of a knitter's life:

When contemplating a chummy, charming knit-in, a few basic rules should see you and your knitting progress socially without restraint.

Be firm. Lunch is unacceptable. It presents an onerous burden on the part of the caterer. If you must make lunch, make a reservation.

Cooking? I think not. Where are your priorities? You are here to knit. Resolve to buy in. Baking merely sets a bad example and encourages the next poor wretch to set aside her stitches for a day before the event to prepare. This is unacceptable. The truly committed knit every day. If you must bake, restrict yourself to one dish only.

Serve only finger food. You can't knit and sit at a table. Everything must be capable of being consumable on neat china plates delicately balanced with only one hand.

Grease, drips and crumbs are the enemy. Ruthlessly cull any food that presents any of these elements.

This makes an afternoon tea the ideal weekend knitting event.

Afternoon Tea

- Fresh cut sandwiches: cucumber & smoked trout; egg & chives; chicken & mayonnaise.
- Mini quiches if you must: leek & goats cheese; ham & gruyère.
- A nice moist cake: sultana, banana, citrus or gingerbread.
- I strongly counsel against scones. They tempt the uncautious knitter to slather on cream and jam, a knitting disaster in the making.
- The ideal biscuit is pfeffeniussen, a hardy Germanic number neatly covered in non-greasy sugar coating. In the same vein you may consider macaroons. Be wary of butterfat shortbread.
- Chocolate is out of the question, particularly in the warmer months. In winter, you may consider hot chocolate.
- The centrepiece should be a bowl of the best strawberries.

Drinks

- Tea: in pots, covered with a tea cosy you either knitted yourself, or can plausibly lie about.
- Coffee: avoid it if you can. Coffee increases tension, and jangling nerves are the bête noire of even stitching.
- Alcohol: champagne only. It rarely stains.

The chic evening knit

Of course, knitting cannot, and should not, be restricted to the weekend. Indeed, such meditative activity practised at the end of a hard day would halve all our health care bills if it were more widely adopted. Knit proudly. You are setting a good example.

But the evening knit-in still requires sustenance and, like a little black dress, catering should be chic, simple and witty.

- No nuts (grease), chips (common) or vegetable sticks (dull).
- Dips drip. Use only spreadable pastes. Crostini crumb, prefer a good baguette or better still, a nice sliced sourdough. Serve with a soft cheese, a creamy blue vein and a nice firm cheddar. Quince paste and sliced apple or pear, in season, make nice additions.
- Soup: served in deep Chinese bowls, only half filled to avoid unpleasant knitting accidents.

Or

- Risotto: zucchini and tomato or mushroom, lemon and basil. To be prepared only as guests are gathering and fixing their own drinks.
- Banish messy salad leaves and dressing and substitue with something forkable. Lightly boil some beans and

dress with walnut oil. Ditto broccoli, broccolini and sugar snap peas.

- Dessert: pecan pie or Portuguese custard tarts.

Drinks

- A cheeky chardy. We are talking quaffing not museum pieces here. White is preferable for its non-staining qualities, but a nice light beaujolais is acceptable for those who must drink red.
- Cocktails: rather an effort but stick with the no-mark white classics if you must: martinis (vodka or gin); gin and tonic; vodka, lime and soda. But make them weak for goodness sake. No knitter needs wobbly stitches.
- Sparkling mineral water.

If knitters are smokers (and they ought not be—smoking while knitting shows a lack of commitment) try to invite them only in the summer months where the event can be held outside. Otherwise, your finely crafted jumper will smell like a jazz club.

The Australian Film Commission (AFC) is housed in downtown Sydney on busy William Street, a short walk from fashionista central Surry Hills. The lobby to the lift is sleek and shiny blond-wood; the AFC reception achingly spare industrial with views across the trendy refitted warehouses of Woolloomooloo.

'Oh you're here!' squeals Fiona from above, carrying a very healthy lunch plate of home-made salad, 'I'll just round the girls up.' I head up the spiral staircase to the Marketing Manager's office, also a knitter, currently away. The girls— Kirsten, Tania, Sally and Rebecca—dribble in and sit down on the twin facing sofas, most clutching a plastic bag, which they sheepishly unpack. It's their knitting. It's not exactly the kind of thing you'd expect from a group of groovy film-industry girls, but there it is. They are all knitters, and they've formed a knitting club at work.

'Oh, I've got to show you what Sabina's doing,' says Fiona Cleverly, Marketing Assistant, rustling around the absent Marketing Manager's chair, 'Look.' She brings over some needles knitted with large loopy stitches in pale wool. 'Peter [Sabina's husband] made the needles from dowel,' she says, 'it made me think, could you use drumsticks?'

Tania Djipalo, Research Officer, pulls out her red scarf and swooshes it around her neck. 'It's my sausage,' she says with a laugh, smoothing the skinny scarf that does indeed curl up like a kransky. 'Stocking stitch,' she says of the curl. 'It just did it.'

'Here's my Cossack hat,' says Sally Tulloch, Industry and Cultural Development Assistant, tossing a square honey-coloured beret onto the table.

'Rebecca's knitting a jumper,' says Tania. Rebecca Mostyn, from Research grins shyly.

'I learnt off a friend last year at a picnic,' says Fiona. 'She's a funky chick. She pulled out her knitting and she'd brought along an extra pair of needles, so we sat there and knitted.'

'How did this club start?' I ask.

'I remember talking with Kirsten,' says Tania vaguely, 'then Sally said she'd like to learn . . . '

'I've always been a bit crafty,' says Sally.

'We began meeting and having regular sessions,' says Tania.

'Then we outed ourselves,' says Kirsten Krauth, Marketing Researcher.

'We had a day out,' says Fiona. 'Rozelle Markets, Herbie's Spices, then off to Champion Textiles. Now we have an email group,' she continues, '<nannas@afc>.'

'Me and Sally are quite competitive,' says Tania.

'I stayed up until 11.30 knitting,' says Sally.

'I stayed up later,' laughs Tania.

'But why the group?' I persist.

'How do people get together nowadays?' says Tania thoughtfully. 'Blokes get together in their sheds or jamming, or they're into cars. I'm new to Sydney and it's hard to meet friends. I like having an outing with the girls.' She laughs again. 'I say to my husband Toby, "I'm going knitting." I think it's a nice thing that women can do together, and we've mostly lost that art.'

Now they've even started doing joint projects, Sally and Rebecca are knitting two scarves with another friend to give as a wedding gift. Fiona is knitting with a group of girls whose husbands and boyfriends are in a band together.

'I just had my ideal Saturday night,' says Sally, 'I cooked my favourite meal and knitted all night.'

None are natives to Sydney. All of the group have come here from somewhere else. 'Melbourne has a lot more cosiness,' says Sally. 'There's less stress in Adelaide,' agrees Tania. 'Here it's all stress. It's the hardest thing to do in our society, nothing. You can't just "be", you have to "do". I'm always counselling people that it's okay to do nothing, it's okay to just sit home and knit. We've got the freedom to do anything in our society and we've lost ourselves in the process.'

'My partner wants me to knit,' says Tania. 'He says I'm calmer. It's like meditation for me.' She looks thoughtful and adds, 'It's a return to the soul. Carl Jung talks about these movements in the world. It's a group consciousness thing. Feminism is all "where do you fit in"—it's about labels—craft is a more soulful thing.'

Knitting Diary, 14 August 2002

Friend Alistair's fortieth Birthday. It's a nautical theme. I'm nervous. My first knitted gift. I make Alistair open the parcel. 'I knitted that,' I say proudly. 'Hey,' he complains pulling out the gift. 'North Melbourne colours.' Alistair, unlike the rest of the State refuses to follow football, yet still has the temerity to point out the AFL colours. Vow never to knit for a Victorian again.

I'm still thinking about Tania and group consciousness when I get invited to a knit-in with Lisa's group. This time it's at Marie's—'Bim's'—narrow neat apartment in Elizabeth Bay. On either side of her loungeroom hang canvases underpainted then strung tight with wide feral knitted swatches. Bim is busy bustling in the kitchen while the others troop in. Lisa convincingly passes off a store-bought dip as homemade as the others open bottles and expertly sip, wine in one hand, knitting out in the other.

There's an easiness between them that goes beyond banter. In their knitting they're all at different levels. Jo is learning to purl left-handed, newbie Karen needs someone to cast her knitting on for her. Lisa is close to finishing a free-form jumper. 'Knit yourself a threesome,' jokes someone. 'Hey, can you get a pattern for that?' shoots back Jo. But the friendship freewheels, the conversation slipping from music festivals, gossip, teaching new stitches, relationships and swapping recipes. All very *Steel Magnolias.*

Looking at it, I can't help thinking that while it's not formally set up like a consciousness-raising—maybe you would have to go to a book club for that—it is, for two solid hours, simply women together talking about life. Easy, friendly, funny. It is, simply, a knitting circle.

Knitting Diary, 10 June 2002
I subscribe to the knitting-Australia knit list on the Internet at <knitting-australia@yahoogroups.com>. It's a

moderated list run by Sharyn and Kerrie-Anne, two self-proclaimed 'list mums'. The first welcoming email invites me to introduce myself. I decide to out myself as a writer as well as a knitter. I tell them about my book.

'I'm not a trendy 30-something, I'm a trendy 50-something, but I really identified with those women. I'm writing crime fiction at the moment and my hero is a 40-something woman who would sometimes prefer to stay home and solve a knitting problem than follow up on a clue. Anyone else relate to that?' says Mary Helen.

' . . . I belong to the NSW Knitters' Guild . . . Life will be good when knitting is placed on its deserved pedestal and not considered an "old ladies" hobby. Once you truly get into the art you will understand what I mean. In the meantime, welcome to this wonderful knitting list and the terrific people that live here,' says Jewel.

'You mean the rich, young yuppies are finally coming down to earth to do what the rest of us have done for years?' jokes Narelle.

Around 70 people are on the knit list. There would be more but list mum Kerrie-Anne ruthlessly kicks off lurkers who fail to post at least once a month. List regulars include Dorothy from the US, in her mid-fifties; Peter, mid-thirties; Maz, in her fifties; Kelly, 29; Kerry, in her twenties; as well as the list mums. They talk about how they got into knitting, then they talk about other crafts. The questions range from the basic, 'How do I count rows of garter stitch?' to directions for machine-washing wool, to reports back from knitting excursions. And always progress reports on what they've knitted. When I went on a trip to Melbourne the list told me where to buy wool. When I finish a scarf the list cheers me on. I get posts every day. Lots of posts: 225 in June, 352 in July, 806 in August. Knitters, like all addicts, are impossible to shut up.

Peter Jobson is the boy of the knit list. I go to meet him with no idea of what a male knitter looks like. In Peter's case he is a tall man with very close-cropped hair and round glasses. He greets me at the reception for his work wearing a blue Royal Botanic Gardens golf shirt. Peter is a systematic botanist, which means he gets to name plants and work on their evolutionary pathways. 'They put up "no knitting" signs at work because of me,' he says with a grin, pointing around from the foyer to a sign in the meeting room. 'They didn't like it in staff meetings.' In fact now at work Peter conducts a 'knitting drop-in' service teaching those who want to learn.

A knitter since he was six, Peter says it runs in the family. 'My maternal grandfather, a sailor, weaved and was artistic

so when I took up knitting my mum was like, "Dad did that."
On my father's side there are also a lot of women who are
heavily involved in knitting or crochet—one grandmother was
known as the "lace lady". My mother encouraged it
something chronic, but she got the best end of that.' He pulls
out his current knitting. 'This is what I'm doing, a baby
blanket—plastic wool,' he says of the blue item, knitted in
practical washable wool. 'And,' he adds, pulling another
project out of his bag, 'I've finished James's [his partner]
jumper. It took me just over a year.' This is knitted item
number 23—Peter keeps a careful tally. 'I've done eighteen
jumpers or vests,' says Peter, 'I give them opus numbers.'

Peter is very out about his knitting, and happily knits on
the train or bus to and from work: 'I just don't care anymore,'
he says, 'that mid-thirties thing. Women always smile at me,
and middle European men always ask me about it—they're
so shocked.' Mind you, Australian manhood seems to cope
admirably with Peter's pursuit. 'I knitted in Kalgoorlie last
year on a field trip,' he says. 'We were there in the hotel and
this bloke came over, and said,'—Peter assumes a lazy outback
drawl—'"Fuck me dead, I've see it all now, a bloke knitting.
What are you making mate?" And I said, "A baby's blanket."
"Well, I'm really impressed," he replied, and that was it.
We were even watching a Chuck Norris film,' laughs Peter,

conceding, 'it might have helped that I had two very good looking girls with me.'

Peter is also one of the most active posters on the knit list. 'That started a year ago,' he says, 'I just typed in "knitting" to see what popped up on the Internet. Americans dominate most lists, but this one is mostly Australian. Kerrie-Anne is in Queensland, Sharyn's in Perth. I wrote to Kerrie-Anne and said "I'm a man, do you have any objections?" And she said, "We'd be thrilled." And I've been embraced ever since.'

'The list is like rural Australia as we remember it,' he says. 'We do want to know what everyone is doing. If you're down in the dumps there's someone there, reading, responding.' He's right. Members often check on the progress of people's sick partners, inquire how the job hunting is going or commiserate in bad times. Open, accepting, caring; just what you want from a community. 'I was very shy about outing myself as gay,' says Peter, 'I did it very slowly, then Judy [on the list] just said "Get on with it, people don't care," and she was right.'

Now he says, 'I have friends all over the country.' Peter loves the BASIS square swap. BASIS stands for 'Brothers And Sisters In Stitches'. It used to be 'SIS' but was changed in Peter's honour. The principle is simple. People on the list are matched each month and they exchange knitted swatches.

Some in the group are making knee rugs, others bags, while some just use them as doilies. Perhaps it's popular for giving a cyber community something demonstratively tangible. Certainly the group does band together, as demonstrated during a bad time for Kerrie-Anne earlier this year.

'The list came to my rescue at the start of the year,' recounts Kerrie-Anne from her home in Gladstone, Queensland. 'My sister was dying with cancer at age 37 and I went to Melbourne to visit her. She passed away eight weeks later. The list knew what was going on and they sent me wishes all the way along. Then someone asked, "Will you be going to the funeral?" and I said, "No, our budget is too tight for that." So then someone sent an email saying, "If 50 people put in $10 we can get Kerrie-Anne to Melbourne." All of a sudden there was this big appeal for me. In the end about a dozen banded together and they got me to Melbourne. I was just amazed at their support.'

Kerrie-Anne sees the Internet as a way of forging a community: 'When we first moved up here to Queensland I guess I relied on the Internet for friendship,' she says. 'I didn't do the playgroup scene because I had friends on the Internet I'd email each day. I guess I'm just a chatty person.'

Between the list, her four kids, her volunteer work at her kids' schools, and an online business making knitting rolls in which to store needles, you wouldn't think Kerrie-Anne would have much time to actually knit, but she maintains she does most days. Currently she's mad about knitting toys, pointing out that in Queensland it doesn't really get cold enough for jumpers. 'Now I'm hooked I've always got something on the go. When my sister was sick and died I did a hell of a lot of knitting. When I'm stressed I'll sit and knit for hours. If I don't want to knit what I'm making I'll just sit and knit a garter stitch square. It's like people who squeeze stress balls. I'd never have thought that two years down the track I'd still be knitting,' she says, 'but all those girls and guys on the Net have really shown the way.'

In her two years' moderating the list she's only had to ask one person to leave because, 'She was over the top, emailing constantly, people were leaving because of her.' 'I was a little bit annoyed recently,' she says, 'with one who just joined to promote her business and didn't even introduce herself. That's all she seems to want to do.' But that's the worst of it. The best? 'They've become like family, some of the members,' she says simply.

CHAPTER FIVE

The
trend setters

Q. *A friend and I started knitting together but now I am more advanced. Is it acceptable for me to begin a jumper when she still hasn't cast off her first scarf?*

A. Ah, women's inhumanity to women makes countless cynics smile. Knitting is not, and should never be a competition sport, yet many a close-knit group of friends has slowly unravelled with this very dilemma. The difficulty, however, lies not only with the advanced knitter, but with the slower knitter as well. Perhaps her week has been a particularly busy one. As a concerned advanced knitter it is best to make light of the situation, bang on about how you had absolutely nothing to do on Saturday night and leave comparisons unspoken. If one is the slow knitter it is gracious to say, 'No, please start without me' if one's friend appears ready to undertake a more ambitious project.

> ### Knitting Diary, 18 July 2002
> *Cunningly discover old 1940s knitting pattern in archives at the State Library when meant to be researching. Take home and begin knitting Dad's scarf in maroon and cream. Very authentic. Pattern says cast on 77 stitches but that seems too many. Cast on 50. Begin knitting. Damn 4 ply—ridiculously slow. Show little progress. Knit obsessively for two hours. At two inches it is clear it is too narrow. Reluctantly undo evening's work.*

It's mid-winter and knitting seems to be everywhere: papers in Melbourne, Perth, Sydney even sunny Brisbane have all run stories on the new trend. And there is one story that especially captures everyone's imagination—pub knitting.

'Knitting Circles are rivalling trivia nights in pubs throughout the country, with a growing number of young people picking up the forgotten art,' begins the article in Sydney's *Sunday Telegraph*, the biggest-selling paper in the country. A photo shows two happy knitters dramatically swathed in hand-knit scarves, beers to the fore, knitting in a city pub. The piece continues, 'Weekly knit nights have started in Sydney and Melbourne bars, with social groups getting together to have a few drinks and knit.'

Women proudly taking up needles in a pub, the bastion of male blokedom. I love it. This is the true inner city groove I've been searching for. The pub pictured is the Cricketer's Arms. 'Oh they're here every Tuesday night,' they say when I call. 'Upstairs, come along.'

The next Tuesday I arrive early, knitting and notepad in hand, and head straight upstairs. The Cricketer's Arms, perched on busy Fitzroy street in Surry Hills, Sydney has been a cool local pub forever and is one of the few in the area that hasn't been over-designed into a fridge-bare box of wood and stainless-steel. It has Guinness on tap, tapas upstairs and cosy fireplaces. This evening, however, upstairs is empty. Not a soul, let alone a knitter, and I'm not game to take out my knitting yet. I head sheepishly back down to the bar to order a wine. A girl carrying a suspiciously large bag is talking to a barmaid downstairs. I take a breath. 'Are you here for the knitting?' I ask. She looks at me blankly. 'No' she says. Before I have a chance to slink away the barmaid looks over at me and says, 'Oh, you're the one.' Apparently pub knitting is on every *second* Tuesday, and this isn't that Tuesday. 'But I rang the girls who organise it,' she continues, 'and they said they'd come down anyway.'

I head back upstairs with my drink, pull out my notebook and wait.

Finally two girls breathlessly tumble up the stairs. 'Hi' begins the dark-haired one with the startlingly broad smile. 'Are you here for the knitting?' Her eyes glint enthusiasm. 'Uh, yeah, I am,' I begin, sighing, 'but first I have an admission to make.' Outing yourself as a writer can be such a drag in the face of such joie de vivre.

'Oh that's fine,' she says happily once I've confessed, 'we love writers. We're publicists.'

'So pub knitting . . . ?' I say.

'Yeah, we started it because we were employed to keep the trend going,' she says, smiling even more broadly.

Damn. Here I was, the sleuthing newshound on the scent of a hot new street trend and what do I find? PR.

'So all the articles . . . ' I begin again.

'That was us,' she says.

Nikki Mumford, Kate Nash and Adam Mumford are Use My Mind, a 'Publicity, Branding, Management' company according to their business cards. They've been engaged by Australian Country Spinners (ACS) to keep the new knitting trend rolling along. ACS are the giants of the business with the biggest part of the industry sewn up with brands like

Patons, Panda and Cleckheaton. Pub knitting is, as it turns out, serious business.

'How long has it been going?' I ask.

'Last week was the first,' says Nikki.

'You should have been here,' says Kate, 'there were heaps. Fifteen, twenty of us.'

'How about the article?' I say, 'It came out the week before last, didn't it?'

'Oh yeah, we had to set that photo up,' said Kate. 'Didn't you recognise me?' The picture shows Kate and a friend of hers posed pretty.

'Wow, was that your knitting?' I ask.

'Um, no,' says Kate, 'My scarf's not that long—I'm still learning.'

Still the journalist who wrote the story came along to learn to knit last week. It seems such a good idea it's impossible not to like it.

When Use My Mind got the contract to push knitting, their first problem was that the story 'knitting is hip again' had already been done. '*Women's Weekly* did it. *Vogue* had it,' Nikki points out, so there was no use pushing that angle. Public relations lives and dies on novelty: no new idea, no airspace or column inches. And the celebrity angle—Julia Roberts knits! Sandra Bullock knits!—had been used last winter. They desperately needed a new inspiration. 'We'd heard about pub knitting and we thought it was so hilarious we didn't even consider it at first,' says Nikki. Then they made a few phone calls to some media. 'We got a big response,' she says. 'When we made a call to a television station and they liked it, we thought, if they like it, everyone will.'

The press release—individually personalised to each journalist—went out shortly afterwards:

Just thought that I would let you know that knitting is so cool it's about to explode across the country!!!! This once Aunty and Granny hobby is fast becoming a socially applauded pastime.

Now I am not one to get caught up with the whole 'Stars that do it' thing . . . but Russell Crowe does it, Gwyneth Paltrow does it, Cameron Diaz does it, Julia Roberts and Uma Thurman swap patterns to do it.

A few knitting enthusiasts in Sydney have taken it to the next level. They have created the 'Pub Knitting Night'. Full of beers, tapas and a whole lot of knitting, these nights are staged once a week at an inner city pub in Sydney. A strong crowd of girls and guys can always be expected.

Kate was scrambled to craft shops around town to buy cheap knitting needles—'Everywhere was sold out'—and Patons supplied patterns and yarn, a photo was done and pub knitting was born.

By the end of this first official week, they've already been covered by the *Sydney Morning Herald*, some websites and radio stations Triple J, 2SM and 2UE. No journalist spills the beans that this is a PR exercise, it's too good an idea to spoil. 'Everyone who talks about it just laughs, but once they've laughed then they want to be involved,' says Nikki.

'It's just spreading out of all proportion,' she continues. 'People are coming to us, it's not us feeding it.'

'It's real word of mouth,' agrees Kate warming up, 'and it's a crack up. "I went to a knitting night at a pub."'

'Young people want funky wools—not your old granny stuff,' says Nikki. 'And Australian Country Spinners have come up with funkier patterns.'

'It's really easy to do,' adds Kate, 'I'm not the most creative person in the world, and its kind of repetitive, it's transportable.'

'You can put in your handbag and take it where you are going,' says Nikki pitching again, 'especially in the inner city, you can do it when you're sitting on a bus, take it to the pub. I reckon once people get into it, they're hooked . . . and I keep telling guys, "It's a great way to pick up" . . . and because beer's involved there's an extra incentive to come. So will we see you next week?' she concludes.

I've been done by a master and I know it. 'Of course,' I say.

Two days later Nikki is on the phone. *The Today Show* want to film us on Friday night,' she says, 'come along.'

By Friday, the *North Shore Times* has run an article on 'The Art Of Cool', *Nine to Five* magazine has 'Winter Warmers' and the *New Weekly* has covered 'The Knitting Squad'. Downstairs the pub is already crowded with after-work drinkers. It's not a designated knitting night so I'm curious to see how many people they manage to rustle up. Ten people as it turns out, are willing to knit on a chilly Friday evening. Nikki is madly running around casting on stitches so everyone has something to knit and they've even found a couple of boys to sit on the edge, needles camera-ready. In the corner is tall and rangy James Thomas, the reporter, taking a sip of beer and practising his piece to camera. Electric cords run along the floor, supporting the heavy duty lighting the camera crew have lugged upstairs, uncharacteristically flooding the normally low-lit room. As soon as James opens his mouth you can see the brief: keep it light, keep it fun. 'It seems like spinning a yarn has broken into the pubs and young people are all stitched up with the winning ways of knitting . . . ' he begins, walking steadily from the bar towards the knitting group. 'No, wait,' he says, consulting with his cameraman, 'Woolly ways or winning ways?' Woolly ways wins for a second take.

Nikki and Kate are in the front ready for their close-up and James strolls over. 'It's a stressful night at the pub I tell you,' says James for the camera, throwing to Nikki as she explains how the group began. 'We heard about it, a couple of girls together,' she begins, 'friends of friends, so we started the group . . . ' She throws in the dating angle, its popularity—'the pub today got ten calls about it'—and rounds off with a 'it's just a really fun thing to do'.

James sets up a joke about tea cosies being popular and clumsily attempts to learn knitting for the camera before making a beeline for the knitting boys.

'So are there advantages for a boy knitting here?' he asks.

'SNAG theory—good for the image,' explains Rob.

'So what do your mates think?' asks James.

Rob points to his mate Nick on the other side of the table.

'And is this working for you?' James ask Nick, with a significant look to the female company nearby.

'Well I can knit,' he replies.

'The night is young,' says James.

'You've got to be a real man to knit,' says Nick.

Suddenly the room is plunged black. No lights anywhere and the pub is dark. The cameraman madly scrambles down the stairs. Packing two 800 watt lights, it's not hard to find the culprit. After several minutes the lights come up and its time for more pictures. Then lights blow again.

Knitting Diary, 20 July 2002

Have to air cigarette smoke out of scarf after pub knitting. Why, why, why did I think knitting another scarf to deadline good idea? Contemplate buying present instead but somehow can't bring self to do it. Can't even buy clothes for self now on such a 'I can make it' jag. Off course make nothing. Winter wardrobe exclusively last year's as result.

The next Tuesday I'm back. The bubbly Kate is perched by the bar downstairs being interviewed by a newspaper reporter. Upstairs there is a promising knitting huddle. Nikki is bustling around making sure anyone who wants to learn gets free wool, needles and written instructions. Tonight she's busy casting on all evening for the beginners. The talk around the table is about quitting smoking. It seems knitting is a good cure. You can't knit and smoke at the same time. Knit and quit, knit and quit is the rhythm.

Around the table are a lot of familiar faces from last Friday's filming. Dark-haired Lorraine, 27, an interior decorator, is knitting a pale blue scarf with the thinnest needles I've seen, a mere 2.5 mm. 'I was taught by my grandmother,' she says, 'but I hadn't knitted until recently. Then I couldn't find a scarf I liked to match a jacket I bought. I'm determined to finish this.' She holds up the finely knitted scarf—currently a couple of feet long—purl and loopy plain alternating in thick bands. 'I usually do a couple of rows in bed before I go to sleep instead of reading a book. It's now my go-to-sleep mechanism.'

'How did you hear about this?' I ask. 'Oh I'm a friend of Cressida,' Lorraine gestures over to another nearby woman. 'She knew I was knitting, so she asked me to come along.'

Cressida, 27, a production manager in the jewellery trade, is knitting a vivid cerise metallic triangle. 'My bikini,' she says happily, 'for New Year's Day. There's a Splash party I'm going to.' Like Lorraine, Cressida's grandmother also taught her to knit. 'I used to make myself toys when I was little,' she says. 'I'd knit dolls' clothes, scarves, anything. Grandma thinks its hilarious I'm knitting a bikini,' she says, 'She's still got a pattern from a bikini she knitted in the 1950s.'

'How did you find out about pub knitting?' I ask.

'Kate started talking about it,' she says. 'So I went out and bought all these knitting needles at a St Vinnie's for 50 cents. I'm knitting a love rug as well,' she adds. 'All my friends are learning to knit now so I'm getting each of them to knit a square. It's daggy, but it's like having an autograph book, and I'll have it when I'm 80.'

Then there is Robbie. Clearly the darling of the group, he's cheeky with a sly wit and obviously a guy who's figured out chicks adore guys who knit—in a puppyish sort of way at least.

'Kate wanted people to come and support this,' he says of his motivation, 'I thought, Why not? Help out, be a rent-a-crowd.' Another friend, I note. 'But,' he continues, 'I also think it's the whole idea of being creative. I've never been good at creating things usually. None of my family know yet,

Knit or Myth #5

KNITTING IS A VIRTUE

By the eighteenth century, knitting was firmly in the hands of the Protestants, so knitting now stood for virtue and frugality. Since Elizabethan times knitting schools had been set up to teach hand-knitting to poor children and teenagers, with children starting as young as four, but now the target was all working poor, and the Poor Laws explicity encouraged the setting up of these schools.

Few extolled the virtues of knitting more than Catherine Cappe, the daughter of a Yorkshire vicar, who in her 1833 memoirs approvingly tells the story of her 72-year-old sister-in-law Mary during her last, and fatal illness. Mary, Catherine applauded, 'would extend her weak, emaciated arms as if knitting, sewing or spinning and still endeavouring to occupy herself with the greatest assiduity'.

Over in Wales where both men and women knitted, the 'noson weu'—a knitting assembly where knitters sociably gathered around the fire in someone's house to be entertained by singing, a harp or listening to an old tale—was pounced on by the religious revivalists. They promptly introduced prayer knitting evenings where religious topics such as original sin and the influence of the Holy Ghost could be discussed. It didn't last. By the end of the nineteenth century, those knitting nights were again all about eating and picking up boys, or picking up the stitches they had pulled out of the needles. And in England, despite the efforts of the Protestant work ethic-oriented Catherine, knitting had almost fatally declined by the end of the eighteenth century, no doubt prompted by the long-delayed arrival of mechanised knitting machines.

apart from my mother who is quite impressed, a bit bemused and probably a bit concerned as well. Bizarrely,' he concludes, 'it's quite a refreshing pastime.' He holds up his knitting with a look that suggest both pride and bemusement. Robbie is clearly in touch with his feminine side. He waves his skinny snake-like creation. 'Then I got drunk one night and came up with a cock-sock and that's what I'm knitting.' Okay, so maybe it's not his feminine side he's accessing. 'It's green and gold, because that's where the drunken idea came from. Winter streaking. You don't get streaking at rugby games because it's three degrees.' He's a practical man too. 'I was working towards the Bledisloe Cup,' he says. 'Sometimes I'm worried I'm going to create a monster.' Then, 'Oh my god, I just realised how that sounds,' says Robbie with a nervous giggle, his hands hiding his face. 'Someone said to me I should get some steel wool and knit myself a Monaro,' he says, recovering, 'But seriously, I'd like to get to the point where I could knit a jumper, I mean wow, actually making something . . .'

That's the problem with knitting. Just when you're ready to write someone off as a bit of a lad having a laugh, they go and say something, well, almost sage. Maybe it doesn't matter how you came to knitting, sooner or later it will hook you anyhow.

But beginning knitting and coming to pub knitting are two different things. As far as I can tell, everyone here is a friend or a friend of a friend of Nikki and Kate.

'How's the campaign going?' I ask Nikki.

'Ten calls Friday, loads today,' she says, 'But no-one's showed up.' She shrugs and says with a resigned optimism. 'We'll just show up next Tuesday. We'll have to keep showing up. From the Sunday *Tele*, there was so much response,' she adds.

'Huge,' says Kate.

'The pub was getting five or six calls a day,' says Nikki, 'and no-one's shown up.'

We're interrupted by a stumbling Irish backpacker, eyes bleary with sentiment.

'My Nan used to knit,' he says.

'You want to learn?' asks Nikki. He nods and waves his mate over. 'Can you cast on?' Nikki says to me, pulling out two sets of needles and some more yarn from her box.

I nod.

'Knit yourself a cock sock,' says Robbie helpfully from across the room. 'Only cast on two inches,' he adds. 'It's winter.'

'It's winter,' echoes the Irishman. I start casting on two inches.

Knitting Diary. 10 September 2002
My brother announces he's quit his job and is going backpacking. In October. Crisis. Immediately dig out the wool I have hoarded from a previous wool-shopping binge and cast on his scarf. He was going to get this for his birthday anyway, but there is no option of giving it half-done now. Damn all these half-finished projects.

All this trend pushing has got me thinking. What started it all really, this revival? The celebrity stories began to appear a couple of years ago. Were they real? I'm speaking with Jo Sharp, an Australian knitting designer based in Western Australia. Jo's biggest market for her patterns and yarn is the US, where knitting has taken off fast.

'When did it happen there?' I ask.

'Oh, about two years ago it really started for me,' she says. 'But you do know all the press came out of one knitting store in Los Angeles—"La Knitterie Parisienne"—it's where all the movie stars go. It's run by this fabulous French woman, Edith, who's very good at feeding the press.'

La Knitterie Parisienne is situated in the heart of Studio City, the suburb in LA where most of the major film studios are. The area is sleek and modern, sporting some of the few high-rises you'll find in a city more famous for its long flat boulevards towered over by waving palms. In the midst of this La Knitterie sports a dramatic red French awning all along its frontage, topped by a merry wave of Christmas lights, the kind popular in LA year round. So famous is the shop that when the BBC came to film a piece on star-spotting in LA they went to just three places: Rodeo Drive, Spago restaurant and La Knitterie Parisienne. Edith Eig moved La Knitterie here from New Jersey seven years ago when, with husband Merrill in tow, she followed her children to Hollywood after they got jobs in the film industry. Pictures show an intense blonde woman with fashionably messy hair and glasses perched on her nose, tape measure slung around her neck.

'Oh, I started the trend,' says Edith down the phone the moment I tell her I'm writing a book on the new knitting. 'When you're here in Hollywood, it can be very lonely, they all come to sit around my table.' One of the features La Knitterie is most renowned for is the big wooden table in the middle of the shop. It has places for eight, and Edith has seats for twelve. 'It's always full,' she says. If you buy wool there, Edith will set you down and teach you to knit, and people regularly bring their work in during the day to just knit in a social environment. La Knitterie is now the largest American retailer for upmarket companies like Rowan and Anny Blatt.

Edith is still full of smart marketing ideas like her 'bees knees parties' where she provides yarn, needles and instructions for party guests who learn to knit. It was reportedly a great success at Camryn Manheim's *The Practice* baby shower, with guests creating enough squares for two baby blankets. 'We don't have kings and queens here,' she says, 'the royalty of America is movie stars. Everyone copies them.' Really copies them. In a newsletter from Berroco, a big American yarn brand, there's a note, 'I just got word from

La Knitterie Parisienne . . . that Debra Messing is knitting three of our Wickenden shawls. She's adding her own personal touch by fringing the long side as well . . .' Berroco then quotes the pattern number so you too can knit like Debra.

On 11 September 2001, recounts Edith, people jammed the shop. 'That day,' she says, 'we were so busy, we didn't stop. People came in for solace. It brought people together so instead of destroying America they are building relationships.' Edith herself decided to tap her celebrity knitters to each contribute a square for a charity quilt to be auctioned online for the benefit of the New York firefighters' families. The two multicoloured rugs—joined by mauve panels—now have contributions from Debra Messing and Megan Mullally, *Will & Grace*; Jennie Garth, *Beverly Hills 90210*; Tyne Daly, *Judging Amy*, *Cagney and Lacy*; C. Thomas Howell, and even a slightly wobbly square by the resident Queen of Hollywood, Elizabeth Taylor.

Knitting Diary, 29 August 2002

Finish Dad's scarf. Found fault in wool and actually had to knot it together to join pieces to finish the end. Know this is bad. Will hide from all expert knitters.

By my third pub knitting night I have the routine down pat. Go to the bar, grab a drink, say hi to Kate downstairs who'll be chatting with tonight's journalist. Go upstairs, talk to Nikki, Kate and their friends. Deal with drunken, nostalgic Irish backpacker . . .

I climb the stairs tonight clutching a very sober mineral water. But dammit, just when I had written this off as nothing but a fun PR campaign, what do I see? Knitters. New knitters. Ones I haven't seen before. Knitters who aren't just friends or family or journalists.

I take up a chair at one table. Next to me is Amy from America who loves Australia except, 'You can only knit three months of the year.' There's Lisa Ryan, who's here because she has two kids and just loves getting out of the house. And Beth, another American, who ran a charity knitting project as part of her two years in Americorps, 'I had all these eighteen-year-old boys knitting while they were watching the football,' she says. That's impressive.

We chat about real knitter issues. Amy just flew back from a holiday to America: 'I rang the airline to see if they'd let me take my knitting on (needles have been banned since September 11) and they said bamboos should be OK, so long as there was a fair amount of work on it.' Anyway, she adds, 'I'd just like to see a terrorist try and take a needle off a knitter. I'd just be no, no, no, I'll just finish the row . . .' I've brought my Nundle shade card, Lisa has one from Bendigo Wool. We talk about relationships. Lisa met her husband, in true *Four Weddings and a Funeral* style, at a wedding. We swap knitting websites. Amy highly recommends <www.getcrafty.com> for the crocheted skulls. All in all a very satisfying knitter evening.

And that's the thing. No matter how cynical you think you can get, something in knitting always sneaks up and surprises you.

Nikki hands me the dossier. From two press releases, personalised for different media outlets, 43 publications, radio stations and television programs have covered the knitting trend. Use My Mind calculates that in three months it raised the editorial equivalent to $70 000 of paid ads, a handy return on the investment made by Australian Country Spinners. 'Hey here's one of my favourites,' she says, pouncing on a torn scrap. 'It's a gay paper, and they just made it up.' The story includes a frightening anecdote about knitting getting set alight by a flaming sambucca cocktail.

But, she adds, 'Since the pub knitting stories came out, the amount of people I've seen in pubs knitting—people have actually read it, said, "That's a good idea" and have taken it on board. No matter how much you read it in the paper, if you can't enjoy it, you won't do it,' Nikki says. 'The sales are proof of that point. When you walk into Spotlight, you just see empty shelves. That's a great sign. After all,' she concludes, 'the important thing is that people keep knitting, not that the pub group keeps going.'

Knitting Diary. 1 September 2002

Father's Day. Press scarf flat to squash out more width. I know, I know. Pressing is very bad but the guilds will not be seeing this scarf. In my defence, the original 1940s pattern said to, okay? Dad unwraps his present. 'Very nice,' he says, holding it up. 'I knitted it myself,' I say, proud as a five-year-old. Dad instantly wraps scarf around his neck. 'That's very good,' he says, 'look.' He is a good giftee. He shall get other knitted gifts.

CHAPTER SIX

Keepers
of the
flame

Q. *I happened to be over at my friend's house checking through her knitting cupboard and I noted there were quite a number of half-finished projects. I gently pointed this out, but she seemed terribly offended that I even looked. Is she not being unnecessarily precious?*

A. I scarcely know where to begin. 'Just checking out the knitting cupboard'—my goodness—a woman's knitting stash is like her love affairs, best hidden where her husband can't find them. Both are only ever suitable for exposure to friends when it's all tidy and neat again. What exactly were you looking for? As for half-finished projects, dear nosy-parker, just as a tidy desk is a sign of a misguided career, for knitters of passion there are no boundaries, no limits; stitched love never truly ends.

While the cosy pub or knitting circle is fine if you want to stay amateur, just knitting at club level, for some people this just isn't enough. These people are achievers, they do good, better, best. They crave more. They want to learn complicated cables, mixed stitches and how to paint with a whole palette of colours. In short, they want to turn pro.

In Tapestry Craft for a second visit I see a sign for a drop-in knitting clinic for just that kind of needy knitter. 'Oh they're here every second Friday' said Albert, 'if you need it, just drop by.' It's economical too, $6 buys you tea, tuition and company. Addict support groups are the same everywhere. I smile. I don't have a problem.

Knitting Diary, 26 July 2002

Panic! I have been knitting Rob's jumper (20 ply wool, big needles, basic pattern) for a couple of weeks and I'm up to the armholes. But now don't understand pattern. It seems to be telling me to decrease on only one side and I don't think I'm trying to create a punk asymmetrial design yet. It's Friday. Maybe one time won't hurt. I pack my knitting passport and gamely travel down.

I'm late and already sixteen women are sitting around the two tables set up down the right side of the room nearest the door. With only a couple of exceptions I am the youngest in the room by twenty years. Still, more people are coming in. Albert is rushing around arranging extra chairs. 'You're back,' he says, recognising me. It's like being in *Cheers*, three visits and you're a regular. Two more people have arrived after me so it's a tight squeeze. People are putting money in a tin, signing a book, prompted by a robust woman wearing a hot-pink singlet who is hustling around organising everyone.

'You sit here,' she instructs me, tapping a chair. 'Now do you have a problem?' I nod. 'Well, take the seat and I'll come over to you shortly.'

Before I have the chance to own up to being a writer she's off. I'm still hesitating when she catches me on her next round. 'Now how is your knitting?' she says. 'Well,' I say, 'first I have a confession. I'm writing a book on knitting. Do you mind me being here?'

'Not at all,' she shoots back, 'you will promote us won't you?'

'Of course,' I say.

'Would you like an introduction?' she says, 'I'm Ann, I can introduce you to the group.'

Ann leads me by the elbow to the edge of the table.

'Everyone, this is Sharon,' she says. 'She's writing a book on knitting and she'd like to talk to you. She's going to come around and spend a bit of time with each of you and if you don't want to talk to her you can just tell her to buzz off. Now,' says Ann, turning to the woman on my left, 'start here.'

Margaret is not quite a founding member: the group is two years old and she's been coming along for twelve months, starting when the group numbered only eight. But she is devoted. 'I come from Bowral in the Southern Highlands,' she explains, 'I catch the 8.30 a.m. train and then the 5.30 p.m. back at night. Two hours each way.'

'That's a long way to come to knit,' I say.

'I come for the company,' she says shrugging, 'and to learn new ways of knitting without having to sew it up. It's a day out from home.'

Margaret has knitted since she was a child, but stopped knitting when she married twenty years ago. 'Then the kids had grown up, one got married, and I couldn't just fiddle around at home,' she explains. 'My friends are surprised. "You knit?" they say, "it costs you more to knit than buy". But,' she adds shaking her head sadly, 'you don't get the pleasure.' I hadn't thought of knitting being daggy for an older generation too, but it is. The thrift of knitting evaporated a decade ago when cheap Chinese hand-knits flooded the stores.

Just then Ann interrupts the buzz that's been building around the tables.

'Excuse me ladies, would you like to look at Hazel's new jumper,' she commands.

'It's for my grandson,' says Hazel holding up a brown jumper with blue stripe detail running across the arms and neck.

'That only took two weeks,' whispers Margaret, 'and she did it on circulars.'

Then I notice that for at least half this group, circular needles are de rigueur. At the far table, nearly everyone is using them. 'Oh yes,' confides Margaret, 'the first thing they taught me is you can knit on a round needle.'

'Look,' says a petite woman with a cheeky face, in the corner waving a small blue knitted sausage, 'one finger took me a whole hour.' Ildy—'named after Ildico, Attila the Hun's wife,' she says with a grin—is attempting her first pair of gloves. At first I think she is knitting in a continental style with needles jammed up under her arm, but later I realise she's paralysed down one side. She's next to Frandy, a spunky Asian woman, who is knitting a striking red jumper with faux fur trim. 'I joined this class because I wanted to knit something I couldn't buy,' says Frandy. 'I've been doing it almost a year now,' she continues, 'It keeps me away from my worries.'

Ildy laughs, 'Don't you think you're also obsessed?'

'Hah,' says Frandy, 'I'm trying to keep myself concentrating, keep my mind away from the troubles I had before . . . '

Before I get a chance to ask more about those troubles, Ann hustles me up to the top table. 'You must talk with these girls,' she instructs. This is the serious knitters' table. The founders' table. The Knitters' Guild table: Ann, Ione, Frances, another Margaret and Hazel are the core group. This clinic is, after all, a special outreach project for the New South Wales Knitters' Guild and these ladies are also here to spread the good word.

Margaret and Hazel, sitting side by side in contrasting orange and mauve blouses, are knitting with circular needles. 'Ann insisted,' they say. This Margaret first came here two years ago wanting to knit a fine 1 ply shawl for her daughter's baby. It was a great success. 'It's been valued at $2000,' she says. ' I have a certificate for that. That's my gift to my grandchild. An heirloom. You think you know it all, but there's always something to learn. That's why we got into the Knitters' Guild.'

'I've known Ione and Ann for 50 years,' says Frances peering at me through her pageboy-cut hair and thick glasses. 'Ann's done a shawl that got second prize in the Easter Show,' she tells me. 'It goes through a wedding ring.' The feisty Ann

very shy and quiet are bailing me up when they have something to say. I'm absolutely in awe of Ildy,' she adds. 'She gives me heart. I'm worried about having a stroke or getting arthritis in my hands.'

Ann would like to have a few words to new knitters about their choice of wool. 'They go in,' she says shaking her head in wonder, 'buy some yarn, beautiful yarn like mohair— usually quite unsuitable to learn to knit with—and they can't see when they've dropped a stitch. It would really help,' she says fixing me firmly, 'if they were encouraged to make a smooth fabric to start with.'

'But,' she adds by way of conclusion, 'there is no right or wrong way of knitting anything.' This elicits a sudden snort from the previously silent Don. 'She starts off with a pattern then she'll decide to do something else,' he says. 'It's never finished off like she started it—I'll have a heart attack if it does.'

A few nights later Ann rings me up. 'Do you know what qivit is?' she asks. 'I've got some wool here with it listed on there.'

'I've never heard of it,' I say.

'Me neither,' says Ann. 'Next time you're doing your research on the Internet could you look it up?'

'Of course,' I say. It's little things like that that make me love knitting. Ann knows how little I know about knitting, but she thinks I can do research. She trusts me. It feels nice. (Research by both of us turns up the fact that qivit is the down of the musk ox.)

Knitting Diary. 9 August 2002

Am late for second drop-in clinic. Today am biting the bullet—will learn to use circular needles. Jumper nearly finished and in a rebellious mood have decided to disregard pattern and do neck in one piece on a circular needle. Go to purchase circular needle. Ann tells me to get 45 cm needle, but only 60 cm ones are available. Margaret predicts I will regret this.

Pull out knitting smugly. Ann takes one look at shoulders and says, 'You haven't done a three needle cast off.' I have never heard of this. She gets other teacher Ione to show me. Ione promptly whips out my needles, starts unpicking. Then does complicated manoeuvres with three needles, which according to her are 'easy'. Haven't a clue what she is doing, but somehow the front and back appear on one needle, then magically, the garment is knit up without shoulder seams. Can't possibly remember how to do this ever again.

> *Still haven't learned circular needles. 'Do I just pick up in a circle and knit around,' I ask at end, trying to copy the others, 'marking the beginning with a little knot of wool in another colour?' Absolutely says Ione, 'It's simple.' Hopefully not as 'simple' as three needle cast off. On way out Ann hands me written instructions. Apparently I'm not only one who can't remember things.*

Finally I'm ready for the big step. A real Knitters' Guild meeting. The Northern Knitting Guild meets all the way up in Warriewood, on the 'insular peninsula' as it's unkindly dubbed, on Sydney's northern beaches. It is the biggest of the city's guilds, and is attended by the knitting clinic gang who assure me the morning teas are legendary. The meeting is in full swing by the time I get there so I try to slink quietly in the back.

'Sharon,' someone is waving to me, 'over here.' Ann has spotted me. It's like being in the family. I am very deep undercover. The room is set up with tables in a classroom U shape, with at least 50 knitters crowding in. Official-looking people are sitting up the top and a white-haired woman is giving what sounds like the secretary's report. Margaret, Hazel and Frances are all here, and Ione is wearing the textured jumper of blues and greens she was knitting just the other week. Around half the women in the room are busily knitting and nearly all are wearing hand-knit jumpers. Some sport embroidered nametags. It's like walking in on a meeting of 70-year-old Girl Guides. I wonder if they give out badges with those famous Achievement Certificates.

'Did anyone watch TV on Thursday?' the woman up the front is asking.

A frisson of excitement runs through the room.

'Oh yes,' exclaims one.

'My son rang me,' says another.

The pub knitting segment has been shown on the *Today Show*, and included some comments from guild members promoting the Knitters' Guild. A woman near me says she feels sorry for young people who haven't got a craft. 'What are they going to do when they retire?' she exclaims. 'All they have is computer skills.'

'You should have seen how they were holding their knitting,' says someone else.

'Did you see what the boy was knitting?' says another

'Peter heater,' sings out a different voice again.

Amused glances are exchanged. Apparently it's not an original idea.

'Rona was a fashion designer,' whispers Ann to me, pointing around the room, as the treasurer's report is given. 'Audrey who has just come in taught Home Economics. Gwen is a knitter, crotcheter, photographer and jewellery maker . . . ' As the library report is made, Ann and I get in trouble for talking.

It's time for Show and Tell and members solemnly get up and show off their finished pieces, projects and innovations while jokes ricochet around the room. 'The stash' is a constant source of amusement—the knitter's dirty wool secrets hidden in cupboards throughout the house. 'Dinner might have been burned, but I finished this jumper,' is another popular theme. Knitting, I am very glad to learn, morally exempts you from having to keep house.

It occurs to me that knitting is the ultimate 'stuff you'.

Dinner can be late, they say, stuff you, I'm knitting.

So my house isn't tidy, stuff you, I'm knitting.

So I haven't saved the world, lost 5 kilos, waxed my legs, stuff you, I'm knitting.

Dammit, I don't just want to learn from these grand-mothers, I want to be them.

Later I meet up with Audrey Dixon at her home in Turramurra that sports an artist's studio at the back, now stuffed with knitting supplies for her sculptural art knits. 'I'm really getting into landscapes,' says Audrey picking up a textured piece, knitted and crocheted in rust-coloured wool, 'this is a real work in progress. I like botanical diagrams, geological strata.' Audrey mixes boucle yarns with garter stitch for ridges, a line of crochet for contrast. In another set of seascapes, anemones and coral rise out of the blue-green background. 'I'm an artist who happens to knit and crochet,' says Audrey—knitting teacher, art knit enthusiast, past president and ticket holder number 33 for the guild, which makes her a founding member.

The guild has had its work cut out for it since the decline of knitting from the mid-1980s. 'The aim of the guild was always to spread the word about the craft,' says Audrey. 'It was a dying art and we wanted to raise its profile. There was also a desire to learn, improve standards, so we taught each other for a while. The membership overall has been a steady 300, which isn't bad considering the distances people travel.'

Audrey presided over the guild in 1996 when it celebrated its ten-year anniversary. With an eye to pushing the limits, and gaining some good publicity, she decided, 'We needed something big.' The ideal showcase was the *Woman's Weekly* Needlecraft Fair in Darling Harbour. 'We picked a theme,' she says with relish, 'The Mad Hatter's Tea Party. Oh you should have seen the expressions,' she says of the initial resistance to knitting the hats, cakes, fruit and teapots that eventuated. 'Oh, I've never knitted that before.' Clearly, resistance was overcome and in the days before the show Audrey's house filled with knitted and crocheted 'hats, tarts, and four dozen heads'. It took three days to assemble and attracted hundreds of admirers, and a swag of press. Clearly the guild has had its adventurous days, but I wonder, driving away, where will the next inspiration come from?

Knitting Diary. 16 August 2002

Am determined that Rob will have jumper to wear this weekend away so I pack up the bits to take in the car with me. As we head out of the city I pull the circular needles from their packet. Surely this can't be too hard? I pick up the stitches around the neck and tie a red mohair marker at the beginning of the row.

Knit obsessively for the five hours it takes to get to our destination. Knit obsessively in the room there. Am reluctantly dragged down to dinner. Still haven't finished neckband. Margaret was right. I'm going crazy with having to keep pushing stitches all the way around the 60 cm needles.

Finish the neckline the next day and start stitching up the sleeve. Sewing is such a bore. After one sleeve I

give up. 'I'll wear it next weekend,' says Rob hopefully,
'can we go out now?'

I spotted Mac, 37, at several of the guild meetings. She was
there at the Northern Guild, then at the Southern, and on the
guild table at a craft show. What attracts a young person to
something like the guild? I wonder. Today, on a brilliant late
winter day in Abbotsford, a water-viewed pocket on its way
up fast in inner-western Sydney, I finally get a chance to ask.
Mac is wearing a blue and white cotton twin set, knitted,
naturally, by her own hand. Her long straight hair is
smoothed down her back and held in place with a band. She
is set up ready for our meeting with a knitting folder (collected
articles and notes) and a largish bag that promises other
projects.

In what's now a familiar story: four years ago Mac started
knitting as stress release. 'I'm not really a party person and
going to clubs doesn't really interest me,' she says. 'Because
my job is so busy I'd have a lot on my mind. I'm sort of an
anxious personality by nature and if I don't have something
to distract me I start thinking too much.' Knitting turned out
to be the perfect distraction. 'Some of my friends are into
different therapies,' she observes, 'and they spend all this

money finding their inner child—I don't see that getting you anywhere—I feel I have the therapy knitting.'

Mac first found the Guild at the big craft fair each June at Darling Harbour. She remembers her first guild meeting: 'I was a bit apprehensive,' she says, of her feelings on first walking into the room, 'and there were mostly old ladies, but I'm comfortable with older women. The first meeting I felt so welcomed—they made such a fuss. They made me draw for the raffle. Someone gave me two books, they gave me their phone numbers. Now I've only missed meetings when I'm overseas. It's like church for me. I give myself projects to do,' she says, her eyes flashing with intensity. 'Challenges. It seems to keep my mind active. Plus there's the finished product.' I can see how the achievement oriented guild would suit Mac—keep learning stitches, techniques, keep pushing yourself. The guilds are very good for self-improvers. Mac averages three to four jumpers a year. She squeezes in her knitting time between work and a TAFE course at night— 'there's an hour between when I get there and when I have class that I can get knitting done'. She also gets to work an hour early and knits then. 'I'm making a jumper now I've designed myself,' she continues with a touch of pride, 'it's my first attempt at design.' She pulls out of her bag a cable rib, on circular needles. 'I've knitted a swatch and measured it to work out the pattern,' she brightens, 'and no seams. All in one piece. I hate sewing, I hate sewing up. Most knitters do.'

Mac has found more than technique in the guilds. She's found a community. 'You learn more than knitting in there,' she continues, 'They all come from different walks of life. A couple of months ago a lady came from the US to conduct a workshop on shawls. She's a court judge in the US. I had a lot of admiration for her. She's a very passionate knitter and very inspiring.' But it's not just knitting inspiration Mac is looking for.

'I'm saving up for when I retire,' she says suddenly, 'Knitting is a good way to save money. I don't spend time wandering around the shops to fill up the time. When I'm around 50 I want to be able to retire,' she says with determination, 'perhaps work part-time and devote myself to my knitting.' She laughs nervously, 'Maybe open up a little wool shop.'

Mac surprised me. I had expected to find the younger members of the guild itching to shake things up, modernise the club, change things. But Mac was looking for something different entirely. She was looking for her future.

Geraldine Thumboo, the newcomer with the much-envied circular needles kit at the knitting clinic, has similar concerns. Geraldine has only lived in Australia for seven years, moving from Singapore with husband Tom for his work, so forging a community is still on her mind. 'Sydney is very modern,' she observes. 'It's that rat race and people think work, work, work, make the money, make the money. But I think there's more to life than just work. You do have to plan your future. In twenty years' time I'll be retirement age', she muses. 'You should have your friends already. Some could be younger, some older, but if you have something like the guild you're in that group. It's common ground. It breaks the ice. The guild is socialising with a purpose.' Retirement planning isn't just about money. Knitting groups—clinics, clubs, pubs—are a friendship bank for the future.

Knitting Diary. 23 August 2002

Finally finish Rob's jumper. Show great discipline in not handing it over for wearing until I've dampened it and pinned it out flat on the ironing board to dry overnight. The guild should be proud of me.

Still, something was bothering me about the guilds. There was something missing. It wasn't the technique, and it wasn't the

socialising. It was, I realised, verve. With the exception of
Mac, Geraldine and a handful of others, the generation that
most of these keepers of the knitting flame belonged to had
them counting grandchildren rather than nights on the town.
And the newbies weren't really changing that. Then I heard
about the Sydney University Knitting Guild. Sounded like just
what I was looking for—funky young things who fiddled
sticks while debating Descartes.

Which is how I found myself on a late winter Tuesday
walking up to a neat renovated Leichhardt terrace to meet the
president. I had, based on one phone conversation, one
newsletter and a tip-off, formed a very clear picture of Louise
in my head: a slight, intense Singaporean student with a wacky
sense of humour that offset a nerdy earnestness. Her knit-ins
were probably conducted with a fervour that scared people.
Which is why, when the short-haired, Celtic-featured, flannel
shirt wearing Louise Loomes (really), mother to baby
Locksley, partner to Justine and indulger of beagles Boska and
Squirt opened the door, I was a little thrown. 'Come through,'
she says, waving me in to meet Locksley—wearing, of course,
a hand-knit Cossack-style baby hat—'You do know it's a joke,
don't you?'

The newsletter should have been the clue. The logo in the
top left corner—a ball of yarn crossed with needles with a

baroque border looks formal. But beneath it is a column 'Purls Before Swine' and beneath that 'Health Report from Dr Kerryn Felts'. Inside you'll find pictures of knitted toilet roll cosies, Aran oven mitts and reports like 'Spring Fever: Knitting with Cat Fur'. But then again, she also runs patterns for premmie babies and penguin jumpers (see chapter seven), and real advice on coping with dye lots:

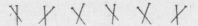

. . . For GenX knitters the dye lot is like the difference between say Tomb Raider 4 and Tomb Raider 5. They tell you it's different but you can't really see it. Well, it's a bit like that for wool colour. My advice is chill about dye lots, if there is a difference you'll be the only one who can notice it and if someone else notices then they're probably not the kind of person you want to hang around with.

Louise works at the University of Sydney, managing the Department of Physiotherapy. She took up knitting a year ago, 'because no-one would knit me anything,' and is self-taught: 'I thought I'd make a jumper, so I read a book and learned how to knit.' Then she took her jumper to work, found another knitter, then another. 'People started emailing each other so we said, "It's a guild,"' she says. Then Louise wrote up a field trip to Champion Textiles and a newsletter was born. Now 80 people look forward to the semi-quarterly newsletters from the guild, which, given Locksley's demands on her time, is pretty much what the club amounts to. And anyhow, 'I don't want to meet these people,' protests Louise, 'some of them are very strange. There's one woman at the university who knits for her dog. She's very dedicated to her dog.'

Public Service Shuffle

(Pattern for a classic skinny tie with square ends)

Row 1. Cast on 8 stitches

Row 2. Knit

Row 3. Purl

Repeat row 2 & 3 four times

Next row: attend counter where six queues of people await you and kindly announce that it is now your lunch break.

Close counter—return from your one-hour break in an hour and 45 minutes

Next: Repeat rows 2 & 3 12 times

Next row: Go home early, you've clearly outdone yourself

Next row: make coffee. Repeat row 2& 3 five times

Morning tea break: Take 10 minutes to discuss your innermost personal issues with your colleagues.

Next row: Repeat row 2 & 3. For those wacky public servants, try adding a second colour. Brown or Beige always works.

Next row: Continue with second colour 4 rows

Next row: Phone a friend. Write personal email. Surf the net.

Next row: Go to lunch. A big lunch will help keep up your strength.

Next row: Repeat row 2&3. If you make a mistake, don't worry, it's always someone else's problem.

Next issue: Public Service restructure. Cast on 300, end up with one.

[USYDknit Guild News Vol. 2, Issue II, 1 August, 2002]

The people who take it seriously are the funniest. 'We mock them,' Louise says unapologetically. And she vigilantly enforces the style police: 'Someone wrote to our newsletter asking if we had a pattern for a knitted koala,' she says, 'No, the answer is no.' Still people keep writing. 'All the letters to the editor are real,' she says, 'Oh, except that one from Rupert Murdoch.' I try to imagine Louise in a real guild. I think she'd implode.

But Louise herself has her own dirty little secret: 'I'm really into quilting,' she confesses, showing me a very cute baby quilt, 'but I can't let the membership know it.' Neat patchwork cushions line her lounge. She might send up the earnestness of it, but Louise is still a serious crafter.

It's been a refreshing change from the earnestness of the guilds. But I wonder, am I missing something? I think of the Mad Hatter's Tea Party that Audrey knitted up. The guilds haven't always been as starchy as they seemed to me. Maybe I'm still looking in the wrong place.

Liz Gemmell knitting classes are highly sought after in Sydney; knitting shops book her for special Saturday sessions and she maintains the riotous bunch at Sydney Community College that saw chronic-fatigued Susannah knit her way to fighting fit.

Observing a class it's not hard to see why she's popular. Liz radiates such enthusiasm for the craft that just watching her is inspiring. Some of her students have followed through her classes for seven years. A former primary school teacher— 'craft got me out of that'—Liz's craft odyssey started twenty years ago, when she and her husband decided to have an adventure. They sold the house and bought a sailing boat, loaded up the two kids (who were eight and nine at the time) and sailed off. On the boat Liz started to knit. 'There wasn't much space,' she says, but she soon became inspired by the new knits Jenny Kee was producing. 'Prior to that all you had were stripes and tacky Fair Isle,' recounts Liz. 'Then Jenny goes and does these spontaneous splotches of colour. Somehow it clicked for me to use graph paper and I started to do it.' Liz wrote a book *Woolly Jumpers*, and four more books soon followed.

In her classes this accumulated knowledge pours out in tips on technique, tradition and trivia.

Liz explaining why circular knitting—'in fact the traditional way'—was stopped in favour of piecemeal: 'Victorian ladies didn't want to knit the peasant way which is why we have front and back and sew together. The fishwives were the ones knitting in the round.'

Liz teaching how to turn a jumper into a cardigan using

a radical cut-and-stitch method: 'You just have to think of it as a piece of fabric—people are horrified by cutting knitting at first, but this is a traditional way as well.'

Liz talking about her own work: 'One of the things I've knitted is a coat,' she says with a twinkle. 'It took six viewings of *Gladiator* to finish it.'

Liz on knitting patterns in general: 'All these Australian books were words, words, words, and no diagrams. One of the things I often tell knitters is the hardest thing about knitting is the language.'

Still, while big in technique, Liz isn't dogmatic about how you arrive there: 'I've got one student who will not put pencil to page to draw ideas, but she can knit them—it's all in her head, in technicolour,' she tells me. 'Whereas another student cannot pick up needles until every stitch is on a graph. It almost doesn't matter what talent you've got, knitting will help you express yourself. The challenge should be—how hard can you push yourself?' I can see why she's so popular.

Today, up the front of the room, Liz displays her latest work—a swinging coat that swoops wide to its edges—while groups of twos and threes cluster around tables chatting, comparing stitches and picking up hints. Val, 66, a businesswoman with her own manufacturing business, is knitting a red jumper for her daughter; Adele, who's retired, is here to learn all the techniques; Annie, who wanted a challenge, is working on a very wild cardigan. Over in the far corner are Frances and Robyn, the bad girls of the group. Frances Stone is nominally retired though she still judges fencing and lectures at the University of the Third Age. Robyn Fallick is a lecturer in Indonesian at the University of New South Wales. 'I've always knitted—it's a precept of utmost virtue,' says Frances, putting on a terribly serious face. 'The class keeps me off the streets and is more fun than the public library. And Liz,' she adds bending in close, 'has some very underhanded tricks and shortcuts to show us.'

'Liz has this thing we should enter into the Royal Easter Show, something like a mohair toilet seat,' says Robyn.

'That will tickle your fancy,' says Liz.

Knitting Diary, 24 August 2002

The big try-out. The sleeves drape down and over Rob's fingers. He hastily rolls up the cuffs. 'See,' he says, holding out his arms, 'perfect.' The night is warm. Rob manfully wears his 20 ply jumper all evening as a light sweat collects on his brow.

My last guild stop occurs purely by accident. I am meant to be visiting the famed Knitting Guild Library in Epping, at the community centre. 'First and third Mondays of the month, 10 a.m. to 4 p.m.' said Margaret down the phone. Pulling into the wide car park I sneak up the back stairs shortcut. I hear them first before I see them. Laughter. Loud, knitty laughter. I have stumbled onto the Epping Knitters' Guild and there is something different about them. I just can't put my finger on it. They look the same, knit the same and are mostly retired just like the other groups.

'I'm writing a book on the new knitters,' I tell the group, 'have you ever had any here?'

'Oh yes, we have a young woman,' says the vivacious Athalee, clearly the ringleader, 'Pia, so we've had our first baby too.'

'A most vivacious young woman,' adds Christina, Athalee's partner in crime. 'She changed our group totally— she had so much enthusiasm.'

'Completely changed my knitting. Now I go feral,' says Athalee with a grin.

Maybe Pia is the key.

Pia Seeto confidently sweeps out of the lift in her office building in Sydney's CBD. I know it's her firstly because she's wearing a funky knitted pink shawl over her suit, and secondly, you can't miss that kind of enthusiasm. I can see why she has her fan club.

'Well, I've always been a knitter,' says Pia, 29, as we settle down to lunch in a tiny trendy hole-in-the-wall café, 'I don't know how much help I'll be.'

'Well,' I start, 'why join a guild?'

'It started really during the Sydney Olympics,' she says, 'I was in the United States on a business trip and someone said, "What are you doing here?" and I thought, Yeah, what am I doing? So I stopped work and had eighteen months off.' Already mother to Phoebe, now four and with baby Isaac soon on the way Pia continued her reassessment. 'I just got the bug in me to actually learn something,' she says, 'give me a bit more confidence.' She began drawing inspiration from her mother-in-law, a Crown prosecutor at the Supreme Court who also sews and who taught her. A knitter since her teens Pia then looked at her heap of UFOs—unfinished objects—and decided to get some technique. I went into a knitting shop and asked about classes,' she says, 'and they said, "You should join a guild." So I joined. When I first walked in, I was the youngest.'

In the year off Pia had in the Guild she knitted several jumpers, a cardigan and a couple of summery tops for herself and kept a journal. 'The guild are good mentors,' she says.

'There is someone to check you, to say you could do that a bit better. I let the guild balance me out with technique. They say, "Hand-made as opposed to home-made." I get a buzz out of that. It's quite empowering if you can get the techniques behind you.

'I find it quite enlightening to spend time with the guild,' she muses. 'You have the quirky interesting stuff, but there's also the whole life thing. When I first joined I learnt all about menopause and hormone replacement therapy and divorces and husbands and retirement—all these types of things you actually get to talk about. Normal women things—I love them. All the girls are terrible housekeepers—good to know. At home the housework might not be done, dinner not done, but it's like, "Fuck off, I'm doing my hobby." We're all great one-pot wonders when it comes to making dinner,' she says with a grin.

Now back at work she doesn't have the chance to go much to the guild, though she's still knitting. Currently she's obsessed by vintage knits and has just finished an outfit for her daughter in two shades of hot pink, knit up from a 1940s pattern. 'I love picking up old patterns, funking it up,' she says, her hands waving animatedly. 'And I'm not a keen fan of unravelling things, so make a feature of things that happen. It's like playing the piano, if you stop people know you made a mistake, but not really if you keep going.'

Pia is feeling her life is back in balance. 'Having all that time off, and having worked, I realised the most important thing you can give to someone is your time,' she says. Now Pia works with her husband and they drop the kids off together. She knits on the train and works a four-day week. 'I learnt from the girls—you only do things that you love,' she says.

I don't know what it is about the Epping Guild that made it seem different. Perhaps it was just the mix of people. All clubs come down to the personalities of those involved. Go to a Liz Gemmell class and you'll walk away enthused about doing something harder or bolder, or go in like Pia, zesty with questions. Somewhere between them is my fantasy model of what can happen. New knitters want to learn from older women. We want to be challenged and learn new skillls. We like to see the possibilities of how our lives can chart in front of us—see the joys and survival of divorce, children, death and taxes. But we want to tell our stories too. In a guild, all knitters are equal. From the minute you sit around the table and pull out the needles you are all there for one reason. To knit. Everything else is exchange: information, technique, stories. At least that's the theory.

Knitting Diary. 25 August 2002

Rob fails to put jumper on. 'You hate it,' I say. 'It's twenty-three degrees,' he protests, 'I wore it last night didn't I?' Husband points instantly drop back to zero. I look at him darkly. He shall wear the jumper all summer.

CHAPTER SEVEN

The
problem
with penguins

Q. *A friend has offered to knit me a jumper. While I appreciate her passion for the craft, I loathe her fashion sense. She's been known to knit koalas into her original designs, for goodness sake. Can I refuse, or if I must accept, do I have any rights in choosing styles or colours?*

A. Having once had an entire original range of orange mohair Arans rejected by my ungrateful family my first instinct is to call you an unworthy philistine. However, in sorrow, I have had to accept that not all share my taste for cutting-edge design, and nothing is worse to a knitter than a gift refused. Perhaps a joint excursion to the knitting store to select wool and pattern is called for. Be tactful and kind. Knitters are not always in control of their habit and she may be in a particularly delicate and manic phase right now. Also consider gently steering her to another outlet. Many charities accept donations of knitted clothes and rugs and you may find they offer the sheltered knitting environment and necessary social supports she needs to help her through this difficult period.

Knitting Diary, 10 July 2002

Baby Kate arrives—first friend's baby born since started knitting. Am filled with smug pride (will hand-knit something) and horror (what?). Have fear of booties and cannot think of what else to make. Extravagantly lie to parents at first infant showing about having begun baby knitting project.

One of the problems with knitting is that after a while, there are only so many scarves and jumpers your family and friends will be polite about. Then you are stuck with an itch to knit, but no-one to knit for. Not to mention the frustration of having a practical skill you want to use for good. Which is why knitting for charity is such a good idea. Or it is, most of the time . . .

Jo Carswell, 48, ecologist, journalist and keen knitter since childhood had a rather good idea in late 1999. 'I heard through the Marine and Coastal Community about the penguins at Phillip Island,' she begins from her home in Primrose Sands, a *SeaChange*-type village south of Hobart, Tasmania. 'They have frequent oil spills and four to five birds a month are affected.' The ranger down there had arranged people to knit these little jumpers which she'd heard about through a British wildlife magazine. They clean the birds and then put the jumpers on them until they're ready to be released into the sea.

'I absolutely love knitting so I thought it was a really cute thing to do,' says Jo. 'I wrote to her and she sent me a pattern. I knitted a few and as it turned out, they were crossing the Tasman back to her when there was that big oil spill down there on New Year's Eve.

'Then,' says Jo modestly, 'I sort of got the notion that we'd need some for Tasmania.' She got together a small group of knitters at the Launceston Library to turn out a few guernseys.

Tasmanian Conservation Trust Newsletter
Number 275 April 2001
'Knitters Invited To Add To The Stockpile'
Most Little Penguins have earned a guernsey after making it through an oil spill. And they need one! The penguins need to be protected from preening themselves and ingesting the oil, before they get their down/feathers washed. There's a bit of a competition going on in Tasmania at present, between north and south, to have a stockpile of

little jumpers to add to the Oil Spill Response Kits that exist in Hobart and Launceston. The Kits were developed by the Parks and Wildlife Service after the Iron Baron spill in the Tamar. Launceston Library staff and volunteers report 170 jumpers pegged on a line in their foyer. Southern knitting coordinators report 75 finished and about 70 pairs of clicking needles in progress.

Meanwhile, another sort of project was unfolding in New South Wales State Parliament House. Marianne Saliba, member for Illawarra, hasn't earned a lot of front-page news, which for a backbench politician is generally a good thing. But she recently earned a plum back-page mention for her behaviour during a question time speech by her honourable leader. Unlike colleagues who were outed slumbering or novel-reading, Saliba was caught knitting.

'Oh yes,' she laughs, when reminded of the article, 'I've had a couple of comments about that.' Looking out her office window across the green of the touch-football-filled Domain she adds, a trifle darkly, 'Comments by people who earned far worse mentions.'

'But what do your colleagues think?' I press.

'I feel,' she says diplomatically, 'that if you work in a male-dominated environment they can look down on it. But knitting is just something that some people like to do. Some people read, or play squash—I knit.' Still, Saliba has compromised: she now knits lower, holding her hands down out of easy eyesight of the press gallery.

'Look,' she says bringing out a white and mauve stripe flat bear in her defence, 'It's a really simple plain stitch and pattern. I hate not using my hands and I can concentrate just as well. Besides, it's for charity.' Saliba was, after all, busted knitting a trauma bear.

The first Trauma Teddy was knitted in 1995 in Campbelltown, in south-western Sydney by Red Cross volunteers assisting children who were in crisis. It was an idea that caught on like wildfire and now Trauma Teddies are distributed through hospitals, fire stations, ambulances, police stations, school sick bays and other emergency centres Australia-wide and internationally.

Trauma Teddy HQ is in the heart of Sydney at the busy Red Cross Central office. The place has an old-fashioned feel about it, with a charity shop downstairs, and volunteers walking the worn lino and carpet upstairs. Like any good volunteer organisation, the office furniture hails from several different eras. It's not hard to spot where the bears live, piled

up around a small cluster of desks near a doorway that leads
in from the lift. Karen Bateman, a cheerful softly-spoken
blonde, is the head bear, responsible for coordinating Trauma
Teddy groups throughout the country.

Moving to an office at the back we push past squishy
garbage bags stuffed full of bears, 200 to a bag, waiting to
be deployed in an emergency. She opens the door to a room
at the end, also stuffed full: 'Floods, Fire, East Timor, 500 to
the States after September 11,' she reels off, 'the bears went
everywhere.' Fire stations and ambulances regularly ring up
to request bears to carry with them in their vehicles. And they
don't just go to kids anymore either: nursing homes take bears
by the bagful, psychiatric wards, legal centres, court houses.
Anywhere, says Karen, that people are sad. 'That's the thing
with the bears,' she says, hugging one, 'they're all about
comfort. They hug you back.' Karen is full of stories: The
child who had a transplant and had to stay perfectly still
which she only managed clinging to her bear; the old lady
who is bedridden and part paralysed, but continues to knit
bears. It is clear that bear love is two-way.

'Is there a colour code?' I ask, pointing to two smaller
blue bags.

'Shhh,' she says, putting a whisper finger to her lips, 'we
don't talk about the ones that might be in a blue bag.'

The blue bags contain the rejects.

Ah yes, there are strict rules for the bears. On arrival bears are checked through a list of no-nos: nothing sewn on that babies could choke on; nothing sharp left in the bear; stuffing hypo-allergenic; correct size, shape and cuddliness. 'Feel this,' she says dragging out a very firm bear from a blue bag. 'See the problem?' Indeed, it's about as comforting as hugging a rock. She's pulling out others: too big, too small, too mohair and something that looks like a trauma worm. 'We take the uniformity seriously,' she says, 'we've patented the Trauma Teddy.' Still, even the rejects are given an honoured place. 'This one was done by a 90-year-old blind lady,' says Karen, holding up a desk favourite. 'She didn't follow the pattern, but the fact she knitted it at all sums up the whole program.' Karen doesn't even know how many knitters there are turning out Trauma Teddies: 'Hundreds,' she says, 'thousands.' Indeed, her books full of just the local coordinators runs to the hundreds. 'We've worked out there are eight hours in each bear,' she says. 'So a whole bag is hundreds of hours of love. You can't sell that.'

It is a matter of Trauma Teddy gospel that you can't buy a bear, you can only be given one. 'I had a call the other day from a woman whose daughter got one in hospital,' says Karen. 'She wants another bear for her son. I said no. I felt a bit mean but the whole point of the Trauma Teddy is you can only have one if you've been through a trauma. Children need that to be special.' So special the bears stay. I leave via the lift clutching my own multi-striped Trauma Teddy. From a blue bag.

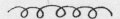

Meanwhile, back in Tasmania, it's penguin not bear love that has the knitters fired up. Having got her Launceston Library knitters saving the penguins Jo decided to use a little of the endemic North–South Taswegian rivalry between Hobart and Launceston in a penguin jumper knit-off. With bit of publicity from the Launceston *Examiner*, the results were a first delivery of 800 penguin jumpers. 'People were knitting like crazy,' she says. 'Then somehow Reuters got hold of it.' The penguins had gone international.

The Tasmanian Conservationist
Number 276 June 2001
Penguin Jumpers Update
The response to the call for penguin jumpers has been, quite simply, overwhelming. By the end of July, an estimated 2800

jumpers have been received, with 50 to 100 still arriving each week. Inquiries and requests for jumper patterns are also still arriving at around five per day. As well as every Australian State participating, jumpers have also arrived from Belgium, Canada, the Czech Republic, Finland, Germany, Italy, Japan, New Zealand, the Netherlands, the UK and the USA. The TCT will shortly be winding up this project, although jumpers are likely to be coming in for some time yet.

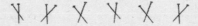

A selection of penguin jumper letters

I read your article about the Penguins and I am willing to knit. I am 86 and legally blind but I'm still capable of knitting. I knit squares for toys and this will be something different to try. Hopefully I can be of some help to the penguins.

From Western Australia

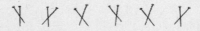

. . . I travel quite a lot for work and an article in the National Post—Toronto, Canada caught my eye. They had a picture of penguins in sweaters and I just had to see what that was all about. I read the article and thought that this would be fun and I could help. There are 2 sweaters (2 packages) that were knitted in both the US and Canada during my travels. I hope they fit OK. Thanks for giving me an interesting story to tell people.

From New Jersey, USA

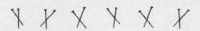

I saw an item about the Little Penguin jumpers on TV here in New Zealand and after finding the pattern on the internet, forwarded it onto my Nana who is a keen knitter. Nana lives in Alexandra in the heart of Central Otago in the South Island of New Zealand. They have been without sun and in the midst of a hoar frost for the last month, perfect weather for sitting inside, keeping warm and knitting.

From Cheshire, England

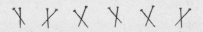

Knit or Myth # 7

RIDING ON THE SHEEP'S BACK

Knitting in all likelihood arrived in Australia on the First Fleet, along with our first industry, prisons, and some sheep that came aboard at Cape Town. As it turned out, the hairy Cape Town sheep travelled well but they didn't multiply and it wasn't until 1797 that the first Spanish Merino was hauled ashore. Its arrival didn't engender the kind of excitement we'd like to imagine. Even as late as the 1820s sheep were prized more for their meat than their mill value.

This attitude began to be challenged with the arrival in 1790 of the aggressive Scottish immigrant John Macarthur. As soon as he could, Macarthur acquired a few of the colony's Merinos and set about a breeding program. Macarthur gets the kudos but in truth, it was his wife Elizabeth who really deserves credit. John was sent back to England in 1801 to face a court martial over a duel. With typical brio he returned four years later in triumph with seven more Merino rams, two ewes and an order granting him more land and convicts to expand his flocks. Spending only a short period of time back here before again be-coming embroiled in political intrigue—which included playing a major role in the Rum Rebellion—he was once more forced back to London for trial. All the while Elizabeth ran the property and became a talented sheep breeder, so much so that by 1819 the Macarthurs ran 6000 sheep.

It was sheep that opened up the continent as flock owners chased the vast grasslands beyond the Blue Mountains. Squatting—new settlers with new sheep pushing out beyond the last pioneer—was the dream, the unwritten rule demanding a minimum of three miles from the nearest other settler. Flocks that numbered 200 or 300 sheep in the 1820s numbered up to 2000 in the 1840s. By 1850 Melbourne was one of the three busiest wool ports in the world.

In the 1840s the first wool crisis hit the industry as world prices fell. In 1843 Henry O'Brien began boiling his sheep on a station that is now cut through by the deadly Hume Highway. Tallow, the main ingredient of cheap soaps and candles, offered better prices for old and diseased sheep than wool. Around four and quarter million sheep were melted down in Australia between 1843 and 1851. From the start the Australian wool industry has been a boom and bust story.

Knitting Diary, 19 August 2002

Have avoided Baby Kate's parents for over a month, as shame-faced about lack of knit gift. But today remember Louise Loome's no-fail Cossack baby hat: get thick, shaggy acrylic wool, knit to a rectangle on largish needles, fold in half and, voila, baby hat! Extra bonus—shaggy wool hides all stitching mistakes. Purchase products in hurried city excursion and cast on on train on way home.

The size of the penguin program is nothing on what Wrap with Love has achieved. Wrap with Love is located on a nondescript industrial estate in the South Sydney suburb of Alexandria. It is open Wednesdays and Fridays and is run by the dynamic Sonia Gidley-King OAM, mother of three, grandmother and founder. 'Welcome to playschool for seniors,' she greets me as I come in the front of the warehouse that is lined with blankets piled up on shelves down one wall and oven-sized stacked boxes down the other. Next to us are 1500 wraps in 100 labelled boxes waiting to go to Hong Kong. While her volunteers in the room next door are answering phones, going through books, and sorting squares Sonia settles down in the sun outside to tell her story. Or at least she settles sporadically, continually jumping up to answer a stream of new deliveries, donations to the door, phone calls and inquiries.

Wrap with Love started with what can only be described as a run of very bad fortune. Sonia had planned a cosy retirement with her husband on Queensland's Gold Coast after a working life in Sydney. Five months into this sun-filled dream her husband started getting sick and didn't get better. Soon after he died Sonia developed trouble with her foot and by the time she got to an orthopedic surgeon her tendons had ruptured and it was another year before she was able to walk. Two weeks after her foot was better she had her second mastectomy. At this point, she recalls, she decided that she was going to, 'Stop counting the years and make the years count.' As she was going in for her operation, 'I said a prayer,' she recalls, '"If I come out, make my life useful."'

Recuperating later at home Sonia sat down to her usual dinner of brandy and dry, cheese, bickies and olives in front of the television. 'This Mozambique disaster came on the idiot box,' she recounts, 'and I'm having an argument with the television. "Someone should do something about that," I said, and a little voice of conscience said to me, "What are *you* going to do?" I had another sip of brandy and dry. It was the first time in my life I responded to that voice. I was propelled out of my comfort zone to my daughter's leftover yarn and I just stood in front of the cupboard like an idiot, and something said to me, "Make a square," then, "Join the squares together and make a rug."' Sonia knitted a square. Then she thought, 'if I've got leftovers, then thousands of knitters in Australia are the same. So it all started with one stitch.'

This was in August 1992. The next Sunday she saw a list in the Sunday papers of the main charitable agencies, starting with World Vision. 'I thought to myself, what have I got to lose?' she laughs, 'I'm over 60, I'll ring them up.' The next weekend she went away to think and came back a with a name 'Wrap with Love' and a mission—blankets would be sent 'anywhere there is cold humanity'. The Monday she got back, 5 September, a letter arrived from World Vision. 'I'll never forget it,' she says with wonder, 'It was saying, "It's a terrific idea. We wish you well, but the transport will be too expensive to get out of Australia."'

'I had this letter,' says Sonia, 'so I rang my friend Fran Aroney and read her the letter. I said to her, "We'll just keep on crafting and we'll leave the transport to providence." Twenty-five minutes later I got a call from Community Aid Abroad.'

'I hear you want to send some rugs to Africa,' said Noel Cowan of CAA, who went on to tell her they had a container going in six weeks' time full of recycled farm equipment, with room for wraps packed around them. 'I went all goosey,' she says rubbing her arms. 'That container was to be the first into Mozambique after the sixteen-year civil war.'

That first shipment went out with 38 wraps made in a month. In February 1993, 229 wraps were sent. In March, after a mention in Column 8 (in the *Sydney Morning Herald*) 1200 wraps arrived in three weeks. According to their records, in ten years Wrap with Love has given away 62 000 wraps. It takes an estimated 150 hours to make a wrap from door to door, so they value the total at over $3 000 000. Blankets have now gone to: Albania, Armenia, Bosnia, Bougainville, Bulgaria, Burma, China, Croatia, East Timor, Fiji, Ghana, Greek Bulgaria, Herzegovina, Hong Kong, India, Japan, Kenya, Latvia, Mongolia, Mozambique, New Zealand, Papua New Guinea, the Philippines, Romania, Russia, Rwanda, Serbia, Tanzania, Thailand, Tibet, Togoland, Uganda, Ukraine, Vanuatu and Zimbabwe, as well as in Australia.

'I believe there is so much negativity in the world, there has to be a positivity,' says Sonia. 'My idea was to keep it as simple as possible. We're now incorporated, but we're not a charity. I've got thousands of little ladies on pensions with limited dollars, and they might buy a four or five dollar ball of wool and they wouldn't dream of asking for a tax deduction. You give because you thinks it's a good idea, not because you think you need to get a payola.'

While Sonia disappears for another phone call, seven boxes arrive from Sister Elizabeth in Corowa, in rural southern New South Wales. Jill is checking the shipment. 'If it says 71 rugs from Sister Elizabeth, it will have 71,' she's telling Helen. Helen brings over a rug to show me. 'It came out of the box with a note,' she says, reading it out. '"This might not be a prize winning rug, but it was knit by a 95-year-old lady." And it's pretty good,' she says, holding out the slightly wobbly knitting. 'Maybe a bit stiff in the joints but that's it.'

Inside, volunteers are sorting piles of squares into equal sizes, and then into bundles of eighteen which someone else can sew up at home. Others are bundling rugs into fives, to be packed into boxes. 'As Sonia says, every one is knitted with love,' says Ella, working knitting up a square. 'I like to knit the kangaroo squares we try to put in the wraps if possible— so people know where they came from.' John brings over the contact book. 'These are just the contacts,' he says, leafing through. 'Each has dozens knitting for them. We have 20 000 to 30 000 people knitting we think. We get 800 to 1000 new inquiries a year.'

'It's like pyramid selling in reverse,' says Sonia, re-appearing.

As I leave, I see her magic. Somehow I have acquired a list of tasks: I will pass the word on to the pub knitting people, pass word on to my contacts in *Age Pension News* and put a note on the online knitting lists.

Knitting Diary. 27 September 2002

With baby knit gift finally complete, I make big deal of inviting parents over to dinner. Cap fits perfectly—baby looks like small demon with peaked horns. Parents say this is in character. Weather is warming rapidly, so pray for cold snap so baby will wear cap at least once.

𐌙 𐌙 𐌢 𐌙 𐌢 𐌙

The Tasmanian Conservationist
Number 277 August 2001
. . . Meanwhile, coverage of the project on Harry's Practice on Channel 7, Audubon Magazine in the USA and BBC Radio in the UK has resulted in a surge of jumpers. At the end of September we estimate that just over 5000 jumpers have been received. We have also initiated the next stage

of the project, which will be to get funding to build culverts and fencing [for penguin safety] along the neck on Bruny Island. A number of knitters in the US have already made donations for this cause.

'The mailman would come in with this huge box full of parcels,' says Jo of the growing penguin jumper stockpile. 'And for each jumper we'd send back a little certificate.' Still, Jo had one more story to place. She put the penguin tale into *Age Pension News*, a free government magazine for all those receiving an age pension or seniors benefit. It ran a story, complete with a photo of a penguin rugged up in a penguin jumper, in its Spring 2001 edition, along with a knitting pattern.

'I knew all these women over 60 who love knitting and always have a little bit of wool scraps tucked away,' says Jo. 'A jumper only takes two or three hours, so it's instant gratification. Elderly ladies don't knit for grandchildren anymore—people want things they can just chuck into the washing machine.' There was a huge response.

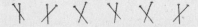

December 2001 Issue Number 279

Penguin Jumper Project Update

The printing of an article in Aged Pension News has provoked a veritable landslide of jumpers at the TCT. Over 3500 jumpers arrived between 15 October and 30 November, pushing the total for the project so far above 9000 . . . We are now publicising the fact that no more jumpers are required. Instead, we are distributing patterns for a soft toy penguin, to be used for fundraising, and a wildlife carer's pouch.

'It really was a lovely project,' says Jo, who has since moved on to greener pastures. 'But eventually Parks and Wildlife said, "Stop, stop, stop, we have no more storage space."'

The final total was over 20 000. I remember the reaction when I first called up the Trust to talk about the project. 'I want to talk to someone about the penguin jumpers,' I said. There was a weary pause down the phone.

'We're not running that project anymore,' said the woman on the other end of the line. 'We've got quite enough.'

'How many?' I asked. There was another sigh. 'Bales,' she said, 'we don't have any more storage space. I mean, they'll all be used for an emergency, but really, please tell people, we have quite enough.'

It got me thinking. Knitting for charity is a funny thing. People may knit with love but a whole other set of reasons go with this: it might be therapy; it might be because they want to make something cute; it could be the only thing they can still do; or perhaps maybe a mental picture of someone cold now wrapped warm that sustains them. But whatever the reason, they're doing it because they have been moved by a story enough to take some action. It's a two-way thing.

Louise Loomes ran a penguin jumper pattern in the Sydney Uni Knitters Guild newsletter one issue and got loads of jumpers. In the next issue she ran a pattern for premmie baby clothes for a nearby hospital. 'The penguins got more,' she observes. 'People did knit the premmie baby clothes, but not with as much vigour. We'd bust penguins out of Woomera,' she says turning to the front page issue of the day, 'I say, "If only we could tip oil over the refugees."'

CHAPTER EIGHT

The slippery slope

Q. *Is it acceptable to withdraw a hand-knit gift if sufficient delight and gratitude is not provided?*

A. When one has spent weeks wrestling a particularly complicated Fair Isle and is greeted only with a half-hearted 'that's nice' as opposed to 'that's sensational' coupled with instant garment modelling, in my opinion the gift is void. In my younger days I excused ungrateful recipients as merely unaware of the effort involved. Today, however, I have been knitting publicly so long there can be no ignorance of my labours. Now I carefully vet the giftees and only bestow upon those who appreciate the true effort involved.

I must provide a note of sympathy for the recipient, however, having also been gifted with original craft items I struggle to hide. There is a line to be drawn if the gift is of the novelty variety—a Christmas theme for instance—in which case all that is required is a quick laugh and a brief model. Likewise, if the knitter fails to provide a garment with sleeves of similar length, or commits other knitting faux pas, while gratitude is always called for, the actual wearing of the garment is not. Beware, however, that gifters become suspicious when jumpers are always 'in the wash' or 'left at a friend's'. In this case there is an obligation to provide a plausible excuse for the non-wearing of the item.

Knitting Diary. 29 June 2002
Have a hot date wool-shopping at the annual Craft Show at the Darling Harbour Convention Centre. New experience as a fresh crafter. Imagine polite stalls set up on trestle tables, some church-fête style knitting and the odd tapestry kit. Experience entirely terrifying. Thousands upon thousands of women stampede stalls selling scrapbooking kits, quilting kits, stamping kits, knitting kits. Constant country music in background. Had no idea!

I meet my first anonymous crafter on the first Tuesday of September in the evening. We are meeting at her terraced house that hugs the train line in a suburb in Sydney's inner west. Once the preserve of working-class Sydney this suburb has led the charge to good café lattes, street planter boxes and quality Asian takeaway. But while the workers now are more white collar than blue collar, the place retains a cosy village atmosphere. Dovima Rykiel—let's call her that—fits the suburb like a glove.

Technically, Dovima is 'out' about being a knitter and she turns out natty hats and socks that are admired in her office.

She even knits in public. 'I first picked up sticks in '97,' she recounts, 'I had a bike accident and had broken my hand and knitting was good for getting back that agility. Now when I get home from a deadline I have to knit something very stupid—very basic. It's much more relaxing than drawing pictures of the people you hate.'

Knitting per se isn't the problem. It's the slippery slope that knitting has led her down. For a start, she spins and dyes her own wool. 'I don't like a lot of the wool you can buy in the shops,' she says by way of explanation, 'and I've always dyed things like my hair.' She was first taught by a friend who sold her a drop spindle she'd had her woodwork students manufacture. Drop spindle is the most basic way of spinning and is still used in the developing world. 'It took me three days to learn,' she says, 'I used every swear word and I invented some, but it's one of those arts—once you get it, you totally get it.' Now she spins anything she can get her hands on. She brings over a peasant hat she's knitted from her own spun wool. 'It's completely waterproof,' she says, 'if you don't mind your head smelling like a sheep.'

Now none of this would matter if Dovima worked as, say, a ranger, but with her career in the image-conscious publishing industry, this look could make or break her next career move. Even so, sheep-smelly hair aside, spinning is unlikely to get her outright dismissed from the styler's bureau. But her next dirty secret just might: Dovima is a medieval re-enactor who goes away for week-long 1500s camps, tutors in medieval knitting and is living with a fellow knight.

'It astonishes me I do this stuff,' she agrees, ' but it's much safer. Otherwise I might join the real world politics like the Greens,' she says, recoiling with horror. 'At least here I look good in the frocks. And,' she adds, 'I would never have learnt to sew or knit or spin, and I would never have met—we'll call him Lancelot—if I hadn't.' Fair point.

'Medieval knitting is fascinating,' she says with the fervour of a true convert. 'The really early stuff is njalbndng— "nalbinding"—which is more like crochet and looks a bit like stockinette. Then you have the beautiful stuff from the twelfth and thirteenth centuries—all knitted silks, very subtle gorgeous dyes. Then you get the late medieval period and knitting really takes off . . . ' She is brimming over with enthusiasm. 'Knitted hose in the sixteenth century was like the miniskirt. It changed fashion,' and, she adds with the authority of someone who knows from first-hand experience, 'silk hose feel great. They just swish on your leg.'

Dovima heads up the hall to her tumble-filled workroom. A line of costumes hangs on the back wall, bags of wool awaiting spinning spill out at the front; and baskets of ribbons, patterns, reams of fabric and projects are all dashed into plastic bags everywhere. She grabs up a stocking she's working in delicate lace stitch on the finest needles you could ever hope to see. 'Do you ever bleed?' I ask, peering at the pin-prick points. 'Only when I started,' she says.

For the record, Dovima now also embroiders, weaves braiding, does tapestry, felts and has undertaken a course in devoré velvet. 'I feel very capable,' she says. 'I was a handicraft moron when I was in kindergarten. Craft is at its heart very egalitarian—anyone can do it—and you get more respect as you get better.'

Craft may be egalitarian, but it is also a slippery slope. The question is, looking at Dovima, does knitting lead to craft? And if so, what does this mean? Are knitters teetering on the edge of a whole craftiness revolution? Will this year's knitters be next year's quilters, beaders or weavers? Are we all about to become overwhelmingly self-sufficient?

I met Amy Barker, 32, at pub knitting. A groover who sometimes wears her hair in pigtails, Amy has a bubbly personality that belies a sharp mind. Originally from Chicago, she studied art and 3D media in downstate Illinois, before training in visual merchandising. Visual merchandising—best known as the art of designing shop windows—is a science of massive proportions in the USA and top visual merchandisers are paid very well to prevent them from being poached by rival stores. Here in Australia, Amy now works in merchandising for Ralph Lauren, and she's mad about all things crafty.

Amy says it's been this way from the start: 'From day one, out of the womb, putting glitter on things,' she says. The child of a single mother with one other sibling, there wasn't much spare money around. Her mother, 'a thrift goddess', always came up with great presents, did crochet and macramé in the 1970s, and, adds Amy, 'knitted mittens in double wool, so thick I couldn't move my hands.' So her first introduction to craft was born of economic necessity, a reality soon fuelled by her ongoing love affair with fashion: 'I couldn't afford what I wanted so Mum taught me to sew.'

'I got really career oriented for a few years in my twenties. I really got caught up in it, having a career, travelling the world,' she says of a now-common commentary. 'I have to thank my husband Rob for getting me back—he does model trains—and he just said, "You know, you should start doing it, you can't beat my nerdiness."'

Amy is in fact a new knitter, taught to knit by her mother-in-law on her last trip back to the States. 'Rob's parents live in Florida,' she recounts. 'So here I am in the middle of summer, learning to knit. Since then we've been emailing back and forth and now she's got back into knitting again. She hadn't knitted for years and my father-in-law is going, "It's all your fault."'

Now she says, 'I'm one of those people who walks into a shop and sees something and says, "I can make that." There was this handbag on *Sex and the City* that I really liked. It was knitted. It cost $295 online and I was like, "Wrong". I can make that.' Amy also makes most of her gifts. 'I prefer that over buying,' she says. 'My brother just got married and at the wedding me and my sister-in-law swapped handmade gifts.'

'I have a lot of Internet friends who are into craft, but not a lot of face to face friends,' she observes, 'but I feel really close to my Internet girlfriends. Some of the girls are fourteen others are in their fifties, and they're all so creative—melting toothbrushes to make bracelets, things like that—all drawn together by the idea of creating things. One of the girls is teaching us to make a handbag out of album covers.' The high-tech world of blogging (posting your own websites) has been a boon to the very low-tech crafters. 'A lot of the girls have websites and you just post directions,' she says of where she gets her inspiration.

Amy's favourite site is <getcrafty.com>. 'It's a funny little site. It's so hard to find craft stuff that isn't hearts and teddy bears.' getcrafty carries patterns for a crochet sushi, recipes for summer drinks, how to knit a bikini and punk feng shui.

'How often do you go online?' I ask.

'Every day,' she admits. 'Isn't that sick? It is a sickness . . .'

Amy is a keen participant on the getcrafty newsboard 'glitter'. 'I am one of the glitterati,' she says. 'My user name is gadgetgirl. I like the idea of melding the two: traditional craft and modern technology. I don't find any difference at all. It's a natural progress of things.'

She also collects vintage craft magazines, mostly found in op shops. 'There is one called '*Golden hands*'—and it's unbelievable,' she says whipping out her PalmPilot. 'Here is my database of the *Golden Hands* issues so I always know what I already have, and here,' she says flashing the screen my way, 'are my knitting patterns. Each row, tick it off as you go so you can knit on the fly.' The new crafters are certainly good at adapting new technologies.

Knitting Diary. 30 June 2002
Still recovering from Craft Fair. Had to be led from quilting display after was found fondling quilt murmuring, 'This can't be too hard, this can't be too hard . . .' Must master knitting first. Accidentally

> *purchased lovely grey mohair scarf kit with special pattern.*

There's something that's been bothering me about this whole craft thing and thinking about the craft show it finally hits me. The teddy bear and bumblebee brigade have the craft thing almost entirely stitched up. Traditional crafts are done almost entirely from kits, which is a good way to learn, but it also guarantees yours looks like everyone elses. There are rules. Blue for boys, pink for girls. It's not bad, but it's not original either. The new crafters I'm talking with wouldn't be seen dead making a kit. They want to be original: Kelley Deal trawls flea markets, swap meets and eBay for vintage wools and never makes the same handbag twice; Amy jumps on the Net to get the latest craft instructions online. Are we ready yet for something original?

'I'm smuggling contraband,' says Sabina Finnern sitting down for a coffee snatched between one business meeting and a film launch. She tosses a pair of blue and grey fuzzy baby booties on the table. They look like perfect miniature socks. Sabina is in a power suit. The marketing manager for the Australian

Film Commission, she spends a good deal of her time selling Australian films overseas and ensuring their profile in Australia. Originally from Germany, she learnt 'handarbeit'—handwork—at school which included knitting, crochet and needlecraft. 'It was part of life,' she says with a shrug, 'You always did something with your hands. Then when we got into our teenage years it was the swinging '70s and even guys got in on the action. I find it amazing now. The girls in the office say "I would like to knit," and I'm like, "You don't know how?"'

Sabina knits by 'picking', a particularly European style which moves the needles, rather than the wool in the way Australians do. Pickers work their needles furiously in little circles and they knit fast. 'I can make a pair of booties in an evening watching the television,' she says. Though these small neat circles aren't so necessary for her current project. 'At the moment I want to see how big I can make the loops,' she muses, husband Peter having made her some sticks out of dowel. I remember how when I met the AFC girls knitting club they excitedly pulled out Sabina's experimental knitting to show me. She is, clearly, an inspiration.

But inspired and inspiring as she is, there are a couple of odd things about Sabina's knitting. For a start, she doesn't wear it. 'I don't wear knitted things,' she says, 'I don't even have knitted scarves.' Today she's wearing a spare black suit and silver designer jewellery. Nor is husband Peter likely to benefit anytime soon. 'I knitted this boyfriend a jumper which he gave back to me when we broke up,' she says, pulling a mournful face. 'There's a sting in getting the jumpers back. I never tried again.'

'Haven't you ever knitted Peter one?' I ask.

'No,' she says with a twinkle, 'Peter's never had one.'

It's the knitting curse. 'Never knit for a man', I've been told, 'or they'll leave you.'

But in fact Sabina doesn't make any clothes. 'My mother used to make clothes. I could never recreate that so that's why I don't do it.' And, she adds, 'I'm not a constant "need to knit" person. Knitting's a winter occupation and there's always lots that I want to do or make. It goes in waves. At the moment if I have a spare day I make cards. That way I can incorporate one with a nappy pin with the booties. I make pictures . . . ' she's reeling off a list, 'I'm also into fleece jumpers—they still look good and you can throw them into the washing machine. I used to make cushion covers, bedsheets. For gifts I always look out for things you can make—Christmas cards, baby blankets, fleece blankets that you can fold into a corner—and forever I've had a set of ideas for lampshades. I never ever have enough time.' Add to that

upholstering furniture and sewing car seat covers and you
have a fair idea of her range.

'I just like the creative expression,' she says. 'I make things.
I think it's the old-fashioned thing: what you design and make
is much more frustrating and satisfying. We've lost that sense
and maybe it's coming back. But I only do it if I think it can't
be replicated out there.' For Sabina, making things is really a
pathway to her real passion—design.

'I adore design,' she says with a sigh. 'I love good design
and new forms. But I express it and re-interpret things like
"of the now". We should knit lampshades. I love making
furniture. There's very copied stuff and very out-there stuff
and I'm aspiring to the out-there.'

Unlike many crafters trying to recapture a cosy time past,
Sabina's looking forward. 'To me fashion is a celebration of
the time and of the now. You recognise it. It's an identity thing,
a demarcation thing. Yes, it is a slavery of the new—when
does a fashion buyer become a fashion victim?—but people
always want to buy the look of the time. Fashion is very close
to expression of what you need around you and an expression
of who you are. Making a comment. Celebrating the now.'

I don't think its any coincidence that Amy and Sabina are
from somewhere else, or, for that matter, that Dovima is in
hiding. It is hard to find a crafter who does something

different. Conventional craft is passionate about rules, rules for doing things, rules for what matches. It's still a skill, but for technique, not design. For the moment, if you want to do something originally crafty, you'll mostly be doing it on your own.

In the USA it's a little different. Go-girl zines like *Bust* and *Venus* are championing all things third-wave feminist including craft. An edition of *Bust* from last year had Gloria Steinem on the cover wearing a hand-made T-shirt bearing the slogan 'F word' (that's F for feminism) and was devoted to 'reconsidering the domestic arts, reconsidering the role of the housewife and all the things that go with it'. A recent issue of *Venus*—its first fashion issue—features funky homecraft with directions for making a tool belt from an old pair of jeans as well as profiles of crafters including Kelley Deal and her handbags. Alongside Kelley is Cat Chow <www.cat_chow.com> a Chicago designer who makes 'wearable art' from all manner of materials like chain mail, Band-Aids and a terrific dress entirely made from one 100-yard zipper. There is also Jenny Hart <www.sublimestitching.com> who embroiders portraits of strippers and singers, as well as selling kits 'guaranteed no holstein cows or teddy bears'; and Djerba Goldfiner <www.reprodepotfabrics.com>, who collects and sells vintage fabrics.

Perhaps the USA has a stronger craft tradition than Australia—and a bigger population—but it also seems to be that one step ahead, where people are exploring the possibility that craft doesn't have to be daggy. That the real folk roots of craft are as much about originality and expressing ideas as technique.

Knitting Diary. 1 September 2002

Barbecue at friends' house. First opportunity to show spoils from knitting trip. 'Oh good,' says Tiff over the phone before we leave, 'I'll wear my jumper to show you. I hate it.' It's the same pattern as Rob's finished jumper. 'Why do you hate it?' I ask. 'I always hate things I make for myself,' she says.

I first see Claire Patterson's work at the big Darling Harbour craft show. Patterson sells fine hand-knit tops, jumpers and cardigans dyed in strong colours. Sharp and fashionable, the stall was a little oasis of style among the kitsch and pastels that dominated the rest of the show.

Claire originally hails from New Zealand, moving over

from Auckland four years ago. She now lives in Bondi in a startlingly tiny flat for someone who hand-dyes her own wool—when she goes to fix us a coffee in the kitchen, she has to move her pots of powder dye that line up alongside the stove. Out on the balcony dyed strips are drying on a clotheshorse. Brilliant balls of yarns are scattered everywhere.

'I've never had an idea of career,' she says of her latest incarnation as knitwear designer, 'When I was a psychologist I'd have people say, "I've been a lawyer for twenty years"— for me that is way too long for anything. I'm not prepared to do anything I'm not passionate about.' Claire started out studying science, was Education Director for Family Planning in New Zealand, and has been a keen Arabic dancer for twenty years. Her knitting business has evolved from selling a handful of waistcoats and jumpers at markets to now, where she has a team of knitters, while she concentrates on developing the colours and designs. 'There's the craft of doing it—the technical ability—and then there's the art of putting the colours together,' she says. 'And then there's the design. Putting together a garment someone will wear. It's really important to distinguish the three and understand the three. I'm a real mix of each of them.'

'I have the utmost respect for women who do the craft thing in terms of what they actually do,' she says, 'but I think it's sad that the art part hasn't been developed in them, or the design part.' As a result, she points out, craft has a horrendous reputation for being twee and uncool. 'It's stifled creativity,' she says, 'they're holding themselves back because of what they think craft is.'

Knitting Diary. 27 August 2002

At the barbecue I've brought my latest booty: Kool-aid green mohair, spun seaweed-like wool and some sample cards. Rob wears his jumper. We arrive. Tiff and her husband Andrew are both wearing hand-knit jumpers, damn their smug little asses. No, no, I'm not going to be competitive here.

Tiff and I pull out the wool. The boys go off to the barbecue. The hosts have disappeared. Is it rude to talk knitting if the hosts don't? Probably. We reluctantly put away the wool.

Marta Cantos has recently opened a shop in East Malvern in Melbourne, on the wayside of busy Dandenong Road. The row of shops it nestles in is becoming a little cosmopolitan strip, with the bakery a few doors up installing a coffee machine and tables. From the outside Marta's shop looks pretty much like any other yarn shop. Walk inside, however, and it's another story.

Stacked in neat white metal crates is as big a riot of colour that you will see this side of India. Skeins in vivid lime green line up alongside desert reds and Mediterraean blues. Blends from subtle yellow to orange, or blue to green whirl together, while others seemingly have every colour of the palette blending to form watercolour woolscapes.

It's a weekend and knitters of all ages are coming through the door in a continuous stream. Marta, clad head to heel in mauve lace and cardigan, spins through the busy shop stopping to help with a colour selection here, offer knitting advice there, chatting with return customers. At the front counter is husband George, an engineer who helps on the weekends. He is later joined by daughter Patricia, a government lawyer, while out back in the workroom is nephew Allen, a chemical engineer Marta has taken on as an informal apprentice. 'He's actually working as a computer programmer at the moment,' says Marta, 'but I can't compete with the wages.'

'I just love Australian wool,' says Chilean-born Marta, now a naturalised Australian. 'I'm in love with my 2 ply—

you can paint with it.' She holds two skeins, one blended in purples and reds, another in beiges and greens and twists them together. All of a sudden a blend that is the colour of the Australian bush emerges. 'I paint with my hands,' she says as she gestures dipping her hands in dyepots and splotching down on the wool.

All the wool in this shop is hand-painted by Marta. 'I couldn't find my colours,' she says simply, 'so I started making them.' Only open since March 2002, her shop has been an instant success though Marta has been selling her wool through markets and other shops for the past twelve years. 'The word of mouth has been the most powerful thing,' says husband George with wonder. 'Marta doesn't advertise in any papers.'

'I'm just coping now with supplying the shop,' agrees Marta, 'I can't produce enough to supply anyone else.'

'Look here,' she says darting over to a basket, 'this is English Leicester—see the lustre in the yarn—or this one here,' she is rummaging in another bin, 'this one here is my favourite.' She twists a blend of four multishades. 'I just like colours,' she says of her motivation. 'I studied colours for fifteen years. I can knit, weave, paint, dye, do multimedia, but I think the basis of everything is colour.'

Marta came to Australia when she was 22, having already

done a fashion design course back home. But then she had her children and put fashion design aside. Once they started growing up Marta went back to design and study, eventually enrolling in a Fine Arts degree at Monash University. 'I couldn't work the colour,' she says, 'I used to be very restricted, but at the beginning of the degree they gave us very good training. Three hundred and sixty colours, we needed to know that pattern. After that there was a beautiful flow to my colours.'

But much as she loves colour, Marta is also fascinated by how conservative people are when they knit. Marta teaches customers to use two different sized needles to knit a scarf, creating a variegated pattern. 'It creates an amazing texture,' she says, 'yet they never thought to try it. A lot of people in Australia are fantastic in the craft,' she observes, 'but in their colours are so conservative.'

Marta herself draws on her South American heritage for inspiration. 'I come from a very vibrant background, I was brought up in a culture with textiles and weaving. I went back to Chile in '99 and studied with the women sitting around a pot on the fire in the middle of a room—it was amazing,' she says. 'This is what the interweaving of cultures does. I come from a very traditional country, people who are vibrant and friendly, and then I come to Australia and get all this knowledge.'

'There is a school of thought about colours for healing power,' she adds. 'Colour affects us so much, it affects us psychologically, it is an aspect in our wellbeing. I can see a real need in people for these vibrant colours. As soon as you see a red rose in the garden your eye is drawn to it. People see these and get so emotional, so touched by the beauty,' she says rubbing a skein. 'I want a sign at the front: "Feel the warm, feel the colours."'

> **Knitting Diary.** 29 August 2002
> *Tiffany calls me on the phone. 'I've just seen the most amazing pattern,' she says. 'It's so complicated I don't understand it at all. I really must make it.' So much for knitting as therapy.*

There are two types of knitting according to the inspirational Liz Gemmell, knitting teacher at large. There's the craft type: 'Where the body learns to do it, and your mind is freed to unsort the tangle of life. The day's events, and life's events all goes through your head. And there's a second kind of knitting.

It's challenging and you're away, every bit of brain space is occupied and when you're done you feel you've been on holidays. I've had some graphics projects, and I would only do ten rows a day and I was so exhausted.'

Liz worries we're not bringing children up to be creative. 'We don't really teach craft in schools,' she says, 'You get sold a kit that has the whole thing. A lot of kids I taught didn't even have a hammer in the house. There were no sewing needles, no nails, no shed. If they don't get anything but a kit, they don't have to think about it.' She thinks it stems from an unhelpful perfectionism. 'I even heard that attitude in primary school. We were doing a papier-mâché exercise and someone said, "Throw it out, we can buy a better one." That all comes from comparing yourself to a machine. There's no pride in workmanship. I want to see beauty and artistic expression, It's not just about being flawless. It's the joy of doing it. I don't sympathise with that perfectionist feeling for craft. Handmade is finessed, but with the rough edges a machine can't duplicate.'

Liz put me on to her knitting inspiration, Tom Moore, with whom she's started conducting workshops. 'Tom talks about rethinking knitting design,' she says. The knitted coats she is now working on are the result of Moore converting her to Japanese designer Issey Miyake. One current project, an

Issey Miyake design, swoops off the shoulders and is knit in an extremely fine aubergine wool—less than 1 ply—on twig-thin needles. 'You are knitting to achieve a final result,' she adds, 'while for a lot of people the end is in the doing of it. So it's doing versus product.'

Tom Moore is an unlikely knitting hero, but then, there are a lot of unlikely things about Tom. Now regarded by those in the business as one of the icons of design and design teaching, he spent his actual career lecturing in Education at the University of New England. Knitting, tapestry and design were meant to be his retirement hobbies.

One of five children, Tom learnt to knit as a child, his widowed mother running a dressmaking business in her house with one of his sisters. As a teenager he made garments for his sisters, including a wedding gown and even today he designs and makes garments for his wife and two daughters. But while Tom had already developed an interest in weaving tapestries, it was his daughter who got him back into knitting. She was studying fashion at the University of Technology in Sydney and she came home with some sketches of knitted design that Tom found very interesting, so, he recounts, 'She said, "You taught me to knit, why don't you knit them?" So I did. I'd been doing a lot of dressmaking at that point, and I got out a book of knitting stitches—Aran—and I knit in red mohair a big jacket for a man. We entered it in the Wool awards and won best menswear design.' It was an auspicious start.

Tom sees the key to his success in his background in dressmaking: 'I wasn't steeped in normal dos and don'ts,' he says. 'I do a lot of "sew and cut" technique. I realised this early on when teaching my younger daughter to knit and she said, "What we're doing is making a piece of material into the shape we want it to be" and I hadn't thought of it that way before.'

Tom sees his calling as teaching knitters to envisage themselves as makers of fabric. He asks his students to see the unique properties of knitted fabric—especially the draping and the comfort—and to build up the style and design through Japanese-inspired ideas of how simple shapes fall off the body.

'Generally the way we approach the body in western society is that the body isn't perfect and we have to improve on its shape,' he says, 'Other cultures see the body as it is. To me it seems that the other cultures approach the body in a way that suits knitted garments. Knitting doesn't suit padding, interfaces, darts, but it does suit simple shapes, draped over the body. It's a softer approach. You don't have to be a size 10 to look smart.' Influenced by Issey Miyake, Yamamoto and Comme de Garcons, Tom says, 'When they get it right, it's brilliant. I encourage my students to leave the credit card at home and go to the most exclusive, upmarket shop and look at the clothes: look at the design, how the garment is constituted, and gather resources and a pool of ideas from that.'

I read his philosophy in the *Australian Hand Weaver and Spinner*: 'I think any development in any creative area takes place in three stages,' he begins:

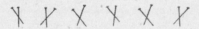

Stage 1

Learning the Basics

How exciting! You have discovered a creative area which really excites and challenges you. The search for information on 'how-to-do-it' begins—lessons, sharing informally, networking, searching the web etc. New ideas, skills and friends are all part of this stage . . .

Uh oh. This sounds familiar. The new obsessiveness, new friends, the failure to make dinner. It is beginning to sound like what the new knitters are experiencing isn't anything new after all. Is it possible I've only been going through a stage? That I was a knitting teenager?

Stage 2
Using and refining those skills.
'Look what I've made.' In this stage your skills are put to use and the 'product' starts to appear. How satisfying to see something in a magazine, gallery or shop and be able to reproduce it . . . Unfortunately, this is where the process stops for many people. NOTE: there is nothing wrong with being a stage 2 person. We all have our own needs and reasons for doing what we do. Stage 2 people keep our crafts alive . . .

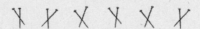

This sounds familiar too. The knitting guilds' jealous preservation and guarding of technique, the workshopping, the knitting classes. People want to get good. But it's the stage three-ers who sound like some of the crafters I've talked to.

Stage 3
Moving Beyond the techniques.
This is the most exciting yet often neglected stage. What can I do now with the skills and experience I have gained? Where do I go? The answer is INTO THE UNKNOWN!! This takes courage—there will always be someone who will say 'What are you going to do with that?' or 'What do you want that for?' or 'What are you making?' and it takes courage to reply, 'I don't know YET. I'm just searching for something but I am not sure what it is.'

To move beyond technique Tom suggests asking yourself four questions:

- 'Can I make this project more individual—more uniquely me?'
- 'What am I going to learn from this project?'
- 'Is there another way of approaching this project?'
- 'Is there another non-traditional material I could use or is there another way I can use traditional materials?'

When Tom himself looks for design influences, he looks very broadly: 'Gardening, pottery, landscape design, anything that has design built into it,' says Tom, 'Don't look at knitting books. I was nearly drummed out of New Zealand when I told them they should burn their knitting books. I was joking of course,' he hastens to add, noting, 'What you've got is a creative mafia—people who guard the borders very closely, what is right, and what is wrong.'

The four lanes of Northbourne Avenue slashed down the middle with a thin strip of green cut straight to the heart of Canberra. Lined both sides with hotels ranging from budget to executive and, closer to town, office blocks, Northbourne Avenue is the road you drive into town and the road you leave on. Peppered on its outer edges are residential houses, some on housing commission estates. It is an unlikely location for art. Unless, of course, you wanted to knit a house-cosy.

Bronwyn Sandland, artist and knitter has decided to wrap up her own house, located on an estate on the Avenue, with one giant oversized tea-cosy. Trained as a sculptor, this 30-year-old has returned to knitting as her preferred medium. 'It came from a frustration with metal and wood, the materials I was using in sculpture,' she says. 'I just started knitting, and I found I could engage with that, talk about the things I wanted to talk about.' Knitting, she points out, comes with baggage like images of grandmothers and tea cosies, so there is already something to talk about.

The house she is wrapping was designed by an architect in the late 1950s and is a classic modernist white box: 'Quite a beautiful minimal design,' says Bronwyn with a nod of her head. 'It's also a public house, part of the utopian vision of Canberra as a city for the people.' But, she says, a utopian design vision is one thing, the reality, somewhat different: 'The design is hot in summer, cold in winter—and getting the police there . . . ' she's shaking her head. Like a lot of public housing, the prevalence of mental health issues and domestic violence on the estate have led to slower police response times.

'The idea of putting the cosy on it, it was about my feelings about the place. A cosy is protecting, nurturing, it has connotations of love and care.' And while she still appreciates her spare, white cube 'like the inside-out of an art gallery', she also digs the irony of putting knitted things onto such a modernist surface.

'I'm exploring ideas of home,' she says. 'I'm knitting the idea of my home and my immediate environment and how I feel about living there: all that noise, all that traffic, people walking past, drunks. Thinking about why I was feeling that way about my home, to me that's the significant thing.'

Knit or Myth #8

ONE'S DUTY

In times of stress and war, people will knit and the war years were certainly good for knitting. At the start of the First World War knitting was actively promoted as an important effort for soldiers on the front line, who at the outbreak of war had few clothing supplies. A patriotic song in the US even had a lonely soldier singing, 'I wonder who's knitting for me'. It was also useful as a way of keeping up morale on the home front, giving anxious wives and mothers somewhere to channel their energies. Knitting eventually become somewhat of a national addiction. The knitting campaign was so successful that by the end of the war soldiers were wiping their dishes with the surplus knitted goods received.

After a knitting period of high fashion in the 1920s—when Chanel designed knitted jumpers, and the Prince of Wales singlehandedly popularised Fair Isle simply by wearing one—knitting returned to the virtues with the Depression of the 1930s. The late Queen Mother (then the Duchess of York) opened up a room in her house for charity knitting. Come the Second World War and knitting swung back to the patriotic. Boys and girls were encouraged to knit long scarves and balaclavas in schools for the war effort and knitting for the armed forces could be done in three colours—air force blue, navy blue and army khaki.

While Bronwyn is busy explaining the dichotomy between the utopian ideal and the lived reality I am distracted by the steady stream of knitters who are calling by her office on the gumleafy campus of the Australian National University to pick up their wool and needles to help knit her project. Marion East is one, her housemate's another and Bronwyn has been on the hustings drumming up knitters on radio because covering one smallish house still requires 150 square metres of fabric.

A neat middle-aged woman comes to the door and knocks. 'Are you Bronwyn? she begins. 'I'm Pat, I rang earlier . . . '

'Oh yes,' says Bronwyn jumping up to a pile of wool over in one corner of her room, 'take your pick . . .'

'Why are you doing this?' I ask Pat.

'Well, I heard it on the radio,' says Pat, 'and I thought, that's something I can do. No-one in the family wants my knitted things anymore, I haven't done it for a long time . . .' Bronwyn is sorting out bright skeins of wool, and Pat selects yellow.

'Eighty stitches loose cast on,' Bronwyn is saying, 'knit for a metre and cast off.'

'Why do people do it?' I ask Bronwyn after Pat has left. She looks puzzled, as if contemplating the question for the first time.

'I think it's something they can be part of,' she begins, 'and it's a simple thing. A guy who works in this office taught himself to knit from a book so he could do it. Plus it's something that people can participate in quite a simple way, but I guess it's kind of wacky too,' she concedes, 'and also creative—you can be part of an art work that is so accessible. People feel they can participate,' she concludes with a nod. Over 70 knitters, from the Australian Capital Territory, Western Australia, Queensland, Victoria and New South Wales so far have agreed.

I keep thinking about what Pat said: 'No-one in my family wants my knitted things.' It's the same thing said about the penguin jumpers, the same thing in the knitting guilds. Knitters and what they're knitting somehow seem to have become separated. The desire to knit is there but the knitting itself is too daggy, or too old-fashioned. Where technical excellence meets bad design, knitters have nowhere to go. There is a well of unloved knitwear too tired, too unfashionable, sitting in silent testament to craft passion gone wrong.

There's an eye-catching picture of Germaine Koh, another artist, at a recent installation of her work. The tiny woman sits atop a long flight of white marble stairs. In each hand she clutches metre-long knitting needles, broomstick thick, while before her an 80-metre river of colour cascades all the way to the floor of the Great Court of the British Museum. *Knitwork* is a piece of art the Canadian began in 1993 as a 'lifelong work'. Since then it has snaked its way through art spaces in Canada, North America, Australia and the United Kingdom, being steadily added to in each location. It's made of cast-off garments—socks, scarves, jumpers—that Germaine reknits into the wide blanket. To date, over 300 garments have found a new home.

Germaine is preoccupied by everyday activities, mundane things that shape our lives. 'From the start it was kind of a terrifying thought,' she says softly, 'what if you decide to do this for the rest of your life? There's a sub-intention to give value to things that are in process and to value that as a thing in itself.' Knitting as lifelong obsession. Not something unfamiliar to many knitters, but not one they would necessarily expect to see honoured in an art gallery as well.

Germaine is fascinated with people's reactions to her work. 'First of all, a lot of people ask me if I'm going for a world record,' she says, 'and I tell them there are plenty of people who knit more than this in a lifetime, they just don't collect it together. You people give a new appreciation for what their mothers have done.'

On the other hand, the professional knitter takes a different approach entirely. 'People who knit—who on the whole tend to be older women—in a way regard it as matter of fact. Often they ask me technical questions and talk to me as a peer. It's very interesting to be approached as part of the club by this group of older women. I've met quite a few knitters who seem surprised someone would immortalise this product.'

With all the wool coming in from donated cast-offs, Germaine also keeps archive pictures of the originals. 'There are associations with different parts of it,' she says, while admitting now some of her memories are growing fuzzy. She sets only a couple of basic rules for the piece: firstly that it be human in scale—it is basically the width of a blanket—

and that once she starts with the unravelled yarn of a particular garment, she must use it all, though the garments may overlap.

As a result, *Knitwork* is visually rich and poetic, with moods that change throughout the piece, shifting from murky greens and browns, to thick bands of colour—bright red, yellow, purple, turquoise, and then painterly mixes of scarlet and emerald, rust and blue, black, orange and white. 'There are variations in the piece,' she says, 'I get tired of combining certain colours, and there is a section I really dislike, but I have to live with that. There are certain variations in stitches. In parts there are details and cables and there are some technical limitations, generally I do a moss stitch.'

'I guess I wanted to argue for valuing the present,' she says with a very Zen sensibility of her ultimate aims, 'rather than dwelling on the past. I think that is somehow related, politically, to focusing on commonalities rather than differences. I think there might be something stoical in this.'

Back in Canberra in October the house-cosy is up. The giant multicoloured patchwork canopy enclosing the house seems to jump out of the landscape, playing with perspective. It is certainly generating considerable interest, becoming a tourist attraction on the busy avenue. Bronwyn is reflecting on the reactions to her piece both by herself and her eventual

115 knitters. I ask her what it's been like living with it. 'Well, it's been a lot quieter in the house for a start,' she says with a smile, 'and through the windows we get these strange coloured glows.'

'For most people it has triggered some kind of nostalgic response,' she remarks. 'It reminds them of a blanket they had growing up. People are also saying it softens the environment, and certainly changes the scale of it.'

'The knitters have been very positive,' she adds, 'they've been coming down to find their square. I was surprised by the number of people willing to participate, that people were so enthusiastic. Everyone's been very positive. We haven't had a critical review yet.' When the boundaries of knitting get pushed out, a lot of people want to come to the party.

CHAPTER NINE

Boom, bust, baby boom

Q. *A friend recently asked me to knit a set of beanies for her family as Christmas gifts. I was immensely flattered at this recognition of my artistry until I found out she intended to pass them off as her own work. As a devoted knitter who spends hours on each personal creation I feel deeply affronted. Am I overreacting?*

A. The scourge of faux knitters is multiplying faster than a rabbit plague and I urge you in the strongest possible terms to resist. I have long been resigned to hostesses attempting to pass off soup and pies from the local deli as their own, but with knitting you must draw the line. They are not merely trying to claim your skill, your design and your craft but also TO TAKE YOUR SOUL. Knitting is a labour of love. The filaments of our very being travel down our fingertips to the wool. She is offering you a bargain of Faustian proportions, for no doubt a paltry payment, and deserves neither your labour nor your affection.

> **Knitting Diary.** 3 September 2002
> *It's 27 degrees outside and it's barely spring. The birds are playing in the yard. The cat is stalking them. Ah, the circle of life. I'm indoors. I'm bored. I'm sick of writing. I'm sick of knitting. Is it over?*

I drive down the arrow-straight Hume Highway which joins Sydney to Melbourne. This is a trip that will take me to both the Holy Grail and Mecca. The Holy Grail is Wangaratta, home of Australia's largest woollen mill for hand-knit yarns, still operating, still profitable after 70 years. Mecca is Bendigo, the legendary in-the-know knitters' paradise where good quality wool can be had for startlingly reasonable prices.

The highway out of the city cuts along into the great grass plains that opened up the country to profit, the birthplace of Australia's great wool industry. Though now instead of sheep there are housing estates as the city pushes out its limits. This year in Australia over 110 million sheep will be shorn, producing around 600 000 tonnes of wool. Australia is still the world's largest producer of wool, earning over two and a half billion dollars from the industry annually. Most of the wool will be exported pretty much as it was shorn. In short, we're still riding on the sheep's back.

I'd been talking with John Macarthur of Purl Harbour. Distantly related 'maybe' to the first John Macarthur, John is a veteran of the wool industry who has lived through at least one turn of the knitting cycle. If you see a hand-knit jumper featured in a magazine, chances are it is credited to Purl Harbour. John was discovered by *Vogue* in the 1980s, selling his jumpers out of the markets, and he's been in business, in one way or another, ever since. An artisan less by design than by 'a comedy of errors', his knitting career began when he was 31, living overseas and needing a sweater, started knitting one. Ever since he's ridden out the knitting booms and busts of the last twenty years.

His shop and workroom are less than a minute from Bondi Beach and the long chequered corridor to his work area is lined with framed magazine tear sheets. 'As seen in *Vogue*' proclaims one, with *Dolly*, *Follow Me*, and *FMG* lining up alongside. The workroom is a picture of organised chaos. Packets of opened wool lie everywhere, balls tumbling out. A shelf of pattern books sits on one end, a knitting machine strung with green-grey mohair on the other. John notes with bemusement, 'With the editorial I get the place sounds like a huge concern. Melbourne people came here and their toes

virtually curl up crossing the floor. They expect it to be slick.'
He says this while working the machine, which he continues
to operate throughout the interview, between jumping up for
customers who come in to buy their commissioned jumpers
or to rat through the ready-to-wear showroom. 'I'm sorry,'
he apologises pushing the machine back and forth. 'I must get
this finished or I won't relax.'

John got into the business in the early 1980s at the heart
of the last cycle. Jenny Kee—who looms large in any story of
knitting over the last 30 years—was startling the scene with
her parrot-bright and patterned 'koalas, kookas and kangas'
knit designs. She and partner Linda Jackson had opened their
store Flamingo Park in 1973 and soon Jenny Kee jumpers
were being seen around Australia. By 1977 the partners had
won the coveted LyreBird Award for Australian Fashion
Innovation. John himself soon expanded beyond the markets
and into the stores. 'Big baggy knits of the late '80s, early
'90s, with tights and a big sweater,' he says of the successful
formula before the fall, 'But once the Jenny Kee thing went
after the '80s people didn't have the money to wear
remarkable clothing.' The knitwear stores started closing,
nearly dragging John under in the process. He stuck around,
kept knitting, got smaller. 'Now it's coming back,' he says
sniffing the wind, 'but more subtle.' In boom and bust

sometimes it's only the small and dogged who survive.

'I'm in a fortunate situation now. I don't submerge myself in directions or trends,' he says, ' I know what I do. I don't care how people perceive it. I do believe I've got a sense of aesthetic. Not just knitting. It's all parts of my life. And because I've got the in with magazines I get fed things—intentionally or not. They'll ring up and say, "Are you doing anything with Lurex singlets?" so I know.'

Still as John can see it coming around again he knows what he would like to do this time. 'My dream, if I could start again, if I were younger, would be to have a knitting concept store: beautifully made garments and design divided into made-to-order and ready-to-wear; accessories—scarves, gloves, hats, homewares, tea cosies—and then knitting wools, needles and patterns.' Those who crested the last wave know the cycle. They can see it but they don't necessarily want to work it. 'I'm at that point of life where I'm not interested in investing that time and energy in it,' says John. He's waiting for the next generation.

Knitting Diary, 4 September 2002
It's not over. Eva arrives for lunch and I show her my newly purchased green mohair. Can't resist. Must knit it

now. The needles I need have half a baby's hat on them. Finish it in the afternoon and cast on the green. Teach myself one-hand cast on out of a book. Very clever. Knit two inches. Did I mention I'm behind on my deadline?

I'm out the city limits. The late winter wattle splotches yellow all the way down the highway. I keep driving south until the wattle gives way to ghost gums. I haven't seen any sheep except the big concrete Merino that looms over a petrol station outside Goulburn. It isn't until I am nearing Gundagai that I see the first small white dots on a pale green hill that is turning slowly yellow with the dry. Soon there are more sprinkled dots, grazing under the great powerlines that web into the horizon. This is Fred Williams country: bare hills lined with felled logs; scatters of sheep thrown on the landscape like children's knuckles; bowling green smooth paddocks that mix stock, rolling above barely running creeks lined with red willows.

I stop in Gundagai for lunch. The woman who runs the tourist information bureau—'fourth generation for this area; my husbands fifth'—lives on a sheep farm. Her husband still runs it but she took this job firstly 'to put the kids through school and uni' and now because she loves it too much to leave. She's a knitter. 'I remember the first jumper I knitted for my husband as a newlywed,' she hoots, 'it reached his knees.' Nowadays she knits bedsocks for her six grand-children. Gundagai has been sheep country, beef country and gold country. But while the sheep and cattle are still in business, thanks to a song about a dog and a tuckerbox, it's now mainly tourist country.

I keep heading south. I'm trying to reach Wangaratta before the mill closes at 4 p.m. Closer into the Riverina the country turns jade green and healthy trees line the rivers. The grasping drought hasn't reached down this far yet.

At 3.30 I finally drive into town, its gateway extravagantly bestowed with signs proclaiming it the 'Jazz Capital of Australia', the winner of a rural pride award and this year also host to the Tidy Towns State Awards. A regional centre and home to 18 000 residents, Wangaratta mixes gold rush era hotels with modern malls. There's a shady riverside park and a plethora of restaurants serving gourmet pizza. But the place is not really tourist-titivated; rather it has a working town air. Wangaratta relies on industries besides tourism for the bulk of its income and in fact a third of its working inhabitants are employed in manufacturing and construction. The Australian Country Spinners Mill, taking on anywhere from around 200 to 400 depending on the business cycle, is a major employer. The mills began spinning in 1923 and haven't stopped since. In recent months they've been running 24 hours a day due to the upswing in demand for knitting yarn.

I arrive at the mill with only fifteen minutes to go. I will have to come back tomorrow. I go to the front desk and explain I'm writing a book on knitting. I want to see the store and get in the factory.

'Oh we never let anyone onto the factory floor,' they say.

'But I'm seeing the Marketing Manager tomorrow,' I protest, shamelessly name-dropping.

'You're more than welcome to see the store,' they say.

Next morning I get to the shop early, just as Carol Collier is setting up. Great bins sit in islands, full of mill roll ends or discontinued dye lines. Around the walls, shelves house bags of bargains: old lines, odds and sods, all to be had at heavily discounted prices. The doors don't officially open until 10 a.m. so with an hour to go Carol is busily bagging great swathes of baby wool as she checks her list of mail orders. She is constantly interrupted by the phones which have been ringing busily since nine. A steady stream of employees passes through the shop and they exchange an easy banter. It's an easiness born of an almost lost phenomenon—the job for life—'He's been here twenty years,' says Carol to me as one walks through, 'she's has been here since she was sixteen.' 'Here's one [yarn] they named after me,' she jokes to someone while sorting another pile, '"Drop Dead Gorgeous".'

Carol has worked at the mills for 27 years. 'I want another eight,' she says, planning ahead to retirement. 'I've also been married 33 years,' she adds, 'you don't find that that often now.' She worked in Shepparton Mills first on the machines, then as a supervisor. When Shepparton was taken over and then closed, she came here and found a job in the shop.

Carol knows a boom when she sees one. 'The knitting industry is really fired up this year with all the Feathers and Fur—the scarf yarns,' she says, referring to two of Patons' most popular yarns. 'This year especially a lot of young women have found the place—they've come in with their mothers and friends.'

On the dot of ten the doors open. People come from a long way to visit the factory shop. One couple from Lightning Ridge are busy piling the counter high with orders, from half the town it seems.

'You're busy,' I say to Carol.

'If I had Feathers they would have knocked you down to get in,' she says shaking her head. This is apparently a slow day.

I start packing up to go, when Carol says, 'Aren't you going on a tour?'

'They wouldn't let me,' I say.

'No,' she says, 'I think they will, I'll ask Michael.'

As it turns out, Michael Hurley, Yarn Manufacturing Manager is going to give me a personal tour. He takes me over to get some earplugs. He's been here just shy of 30 years. 'Just so you know,' he says, 'we never give tours, so don't write that we do.' Maybe I hung around long enough so they didn't know what else to do with me, but I pop the disposable yellow tubes into my ears and quickly nod before they change their minds. For the record, the mill at Wangaratta is not open for tours.

We walk outside the admin block and along the long buildings at the back. Around the corner and I can hear the first clacking of machinery. 'We process wool here,' Michael is telling me, pushing through the clear rubber doors, 'we don't process cotton. We're a long staple spinning operations.' Seventy per cent of the wool produced here is for hand-knitting.

On the factory floor it's like a Willy Wonka factory for knitaholics. Large whirls of cream-coloured yarn looking like giant vats of Whippy ice cream stand alongside shed-long machines, which are gently pulling the whirls into smaller and smaller ropes. These feed into rollers that stretch the ropes again thinner and smaller. Shiny green and cream machines are spinning a thread canopy overhead. 'They're only eighteen months old,' confirms Michael, stopping a roller to demonstrate. 'This is the actual spinning stage,' he says, expertly winding a line of thread back on, instinctively dodging the automated vacuum that runs back and forth along the long line sucking up the floaty wool fluff. Over the next row bobbins that look like milk bottles are wobbling along. The smell is woolly, the fleece having just come out of a steaming chamber, which runs in a big U shape. Moving along the rows of spinning bobbins Michael stops one and makes a tear. 'See,' he says as the machine kicks into action, 'sensors pick up the fault.' A neat rethreading and the machine splices the tear and then rechecks its work. All round the edge of the factory are large bins full of raw materials and more ice cream whirls.

We push through into the dye halls, which have the same sharp smell as a cheese factory. 'There are four ways of dyeing,' Michael is saying as we head past some big bales of spun wool waiting for colour. 'Gusto,' I say, picking up their popular 20 ply. Michael nods, 'For Gusto there are actually three different fibres,' he says, 'up to five different shades.'

This man knows his yarns. I am mesmerised by the coloured hanks coming out of one of the vats.

Past big metal boxes of rainbow skeins he stops. 'Most are assembled on a big wheel,' he is saying, stopping one purple-clad circle and turning it to find the centre of the hank while down the end a machine is stamping wool, pulling it along, stamping it again. 'The last way to colour wool,' Michael says nodding at the stamper. 'Printing.'

The next room is for deluxe wool. 'Fancy Twisting,' says the sign on one bin. Sometimes the mill workers experiment with the yarns themselves, and show the results to the designers when they come up from Melbourne. 'They've sometimes used our ideas,' he says, 'even our mistakes.' It reminds me of the legend of Post-it notes. The 3M company encourages all employees to be inventors. One came up with a re-stickable glue . . . and the rest is Post-it note history. Same atmosphere here.

Final stop is the baling area. This is where cones of the finished wool are spun and packaged into balls. Over one side, large pink hanks are wound onto a giant mandrill that spins out a pink canopy of fairy floss threads overhead. Another set of machines is making the standard oblong balls, while another, further along takes the oblong and squashes it flat. 'Marketing,' explains Michael. Flat balls look more exclusive. At the end of the tour Michael is pointing to the final machine. 'I was trained on that when I first started,' he says, '29 years ago. My first job was running the spinning machines.' I leave via the shop and find when I get to the car that I've accidentally acquired around a sheeps-worth of wool. Well, the mill has been running overtime.

Knitting Diary. 14 September 2002

My new cardigan is looking great. I have knitted as far as the armholes on the back already. I love this plain knitting. My brother's scarf on the other hand, languishes half-done. Vile rib stitch. Vile. Am so bored with it.

Jo Sharp, 43, is a Perth-based knitwear designer who is currently revelling in her new premises with the perfect location: 'A lovely big new restored warehouse in Fremantle,' she says, 'close to a good café.'

Jo has been in the business since 1993 when she launched her first collection on the back of a commitment by retail giant David Jones to the new label. Before that she was an exhibited artist and had opened her own restaurant.

Originally Jo got interested in knitting when she wanted to put some of her painting designs onto her jumpers. 'At the time I remember the thing that triggered my interest in knitting was the feeling I got looking at the knitwear that was in fashion and it gave me a bit of a thrill,' she says. 'I am passionate about colour. I was playing with knitting stuff, and I thought, maybe I can do knitting full time.' Her first garment was displayed in her restaurant where it sold to a regular customer. After that, Jo and her husband sold the restaurant and devoted their resources to the garment business.

'Little did I know,' she says with a laugh. A business mentor helped her do the numbers and she soon worked out she'd never make a dollar selling the finished garments so instead she decided to focus on developing designs and books. 'When I entered the industry it was quite sad and drab,' she remarks, noting that that in her decade she's seen a big shift. 'Now, it feels really contemporary. But at the time I couldn't get any subtlety in colours, which is why I started with making the wool.'

Jo hasn't just been helped by her sense of design, however, and a fair amount of business acumen has gone into keeping the label alive and profitable. 'I think I have an enterprising spirit,' she says. 'My whole family—there are four siblings— we're all in business. I don't think my creativity is independent of what I do on paper. I'm very good finding what people's skill are and putting them together.' She is also good at giving things away. In the past Sharp has done it all—the designs, the photography, the layout. Now she is working with another designer and is looking to hand on the photography.

None of which is to say it hasn't been a rocky decade: three years after first getting her David Jones contracts, DJs closed their yarn departments. 'We nearly went broke,' says Sharp, 'I went onto no salary for a year and we spent everything we had getting me to Canada, which we thought was a stepping stone to the States. Then six US distributors said no.' Finally, in late 1995 they got their breakthrough. 'The US rang and within a month of that call we had the biggest order we'd ever had. If that hadn't happened I don't think we'd be here.'

Last December 2001 Jo moved distributors again to a company based in New York who offered her a huge expansion of her lines. 'We'd based our whole business until six months ago on one yarn,' she says, ' our old DK (8 ply) in 60 colours. Now suddenly we've moved into a different arena. We are working to seasons more. By next year we'll have ten different yarns, cotton, silk, cashmere, coming out of Italy. We're doing ten times the turnover we were doing. We met them at Christmas and by June we'd brought out four collections. Now we're working on summer and next winter. But it's exciting now. The business is more exciting than it was. I'm putting my next decade into it. There's definitely going to be five big years.'

But while Jo is plotting her next onslaught on the world market, I turn inland. Wide straight roads lead you across Victoria, eventually past an Italianate fountain straight into Bendigo, a buzzing inland city that has enjoyed good fortune by anyone's assessment. Thanks to the gold rush 150 years ago it sports an imposing post office, impressive law courts and a clutch of tall churches all built with the opulent flamboyance gold fever brings. Bendigo hasn't got the boom–bust feel of a lot of inland towns that found gold then nothing else and are slowly, inelegantly decaying. Instead Bendigo is a regional powerhouse with its own bank and a strong manufacturing centre.

I'm here to visit Bendigo Mills, the darling of the knitting set. Hang around the knitting guilds for five minutes, and the online knit lists only a bit longer and you'll soon hear about Bendigo. When the department stores closed their wool divisions in the last knitting bust, procuring wool became a serious business for knitters. The Spotlights and Lincrafts and small knitting shops filled some of the gap, but the quest for a dependable supply of quality knitting yarn for a reasonable

price was on in earnest. Bendigo is what they found. A small
family-run manufacturer that sells direct to the public, largely
by mail order. Its shade card—a neat folded A4 cardboard
loaded with tidy wisps from its 'Colonial', 'Harmony',
'Mohair', 'Aran', 'Baby Wool', 'Classic', 'Alpaca' and 'Rustic'
ranges is sent out promptly and orders are promptly delivered.
Most legendary of all is the back room at the factory shop.
Here bargains of great legend are reputed to be had. Not that
this Aladdin's cave of wonder is necessarily easy to find. At the
tourist office there is a small brochure about Bendigo Mills,
but clearly the city doesn't rely on it as a tourist attraction.
'Oh yes,' says the woman in the tourist bureau, 'follow the
tramway out towards the tramway museum, then take the
next street along.'

First impressions of this knitting mecca are that it disguises
itself well in surprisingly modest surrounds. The Mill shop is
down the far end of a red brick building fronted by a grey
asphalt car park. Small and orderly and designed with
practicality in mind, the shop is prosaically fitted out for the
serious knitter, right down to handy knitted swatches of yarn
hanging from each bin of 200 g balls. A customer at the desk
is explaining that usually they handspin this colour, but maybe
they'll buy ready-done this time.

I head straight to the playroom out the back. This is

definitely where the real bargains are. I see Rob's next jumper immediately—a maroon and blue twist 'red tweed'. A bag with enough to knit a jumper is selling today for $45.

But after another turn around the back room for luck I wonder what else to do. ' How busy do you get?' I ask the woman on the front counter.

'We once had six buses in one day,' she says, her eyes opening a little wider, 'I had to sit down when I got home, I can tell you.' A couple of senior knitters are poking around the shop.

'Do you have many young knitters coming in?' I try.

'Oh, sometimes they'll come in with a mother or a grandmother,' she says, 'we're really primarily mail order.' Later they tell me their customer base is the over-fifties.

As far as I can tell they're as busy as they ever have been, but I don't know if the new knitter has been charging through their doors. I feel a little flat. It's not their wool—Bendigo does very good wool, in very good colours. But then I realise it. The clues were there all along: the country-comfort shade card with colours named either for king: 'Imperial', 'Regency', 'Prussian'; or country: 'kingfisher', 'eucalypt'. The brochure from the tourist bureau featuring school-fete style knitting— Arans and tricky baby layettes in pastel wool colours. This is the old knitting. This is the knitting that kept going through the last knitting bust. The knitting of the true believers. The solid, dependable, what-your-grandmother-would-make and you-would-never-wear knitting. Bendigo does put on a major wool and craft show every year which showcases craft designs, so maybe they save the pizzazz for then. In the shop though, it's strictly traditional.

Knitting Diary, 26th September 2002

My brother's birthday and only a fortnight before he goes backpacking. I finally finish his scarf on the way to his birthday dinner, pulling through the tassels in the car. 'I'm sure you can guess,' I say handing him a suspiciously soft parcel. 'No,' he says. Have I misread all the hints about how cold the European winter is? 'That's fantastic,' he says, ensuring further knit gifts. 'Aren't you clever,' says Mum, 'now you have to knit me one.' Maybe, with the orders piling up, this isn't such a relaxing hobby after all.

I finally drive into Melbourne for a meeting with John Albert and Heather Granger from Australian Country Spinners. John is the marketing manager and Heather is the chief designer.

The office is on a busy street-front in Kew, a nice leafy middle-class suburb in Melbourne that has a tram stop, a good baker and some warm pubs.

Coming up the stairs I enter a workspace of managed chaos. 'You can't divulge a thing you see,' says John conspiratorially, 'next year's range.' Samples and knitting are scattered about the room and in boxes, and they have to clear a space on the large wood table near the front stairwell. 'That's okay, I've seen the factory,' I say. John stops and looks at me. 'What on earth did you do?' he says. 'No-one's allowed in the factory.' He hesitates a moment. 'Well, since you've seen that we can show you these,' he says, handing over next year's sample cards, 'because now we'll have to kill you.' Well, the new colours and lush textures are to die for.

Behind John, phones are constantly ringing and boxes are packaged for a display. 'People are going insane,' he says cheerfully, 'lots of tension, lots of conflict.' John, it has to be said, manages both with ease. One of the peculiarities of his job is that Patons and Cleckheaton are competitors, and they have only been married in the one company a few years. 'How do you manage that?' I ask. 'I think I'm going mad actually,' he says with a grin, 'we keep it confidential. You leave yourself open if you don't feel the need for competition. But the brands are different,' he continues, 'with different points in the

Knit or Myth #9
THE WOOL STOCKPILE AND
ONE LAST GREAT MYTH

In 1970 an attempt in Australia was made to even out market forces by establishing the Wool Reserve Price Scheme. By setting a floor price for wool, the scheme guaranteed wool producers a minimum price per bale. It worked for a while until the floor price was set at a level higher than the marketplace wanted to pay, leaving the Australian Wool Corporation to buy the bales. By 1991 the scheme collapsed under the weight of 4.7 million bales of wool, and a government debt of $3.4 billion. Which of course kept wool prices low as buyers knew there was a stockpiled glut. The pile avoided being burned, buried or dumped at sea—as plenty favoured—and the wool was slowly sold off. Only in 2002 was the final bale symbolically handed over to the National Wool Museum in Geelong.

There is one last knit myth that needs debunking. Knitters love anyone who espouses their art and online groups are full of gossip about well-known knitters. Julia Roberts is a cert. Sandra Bullock also. But one of the most tantalising is Russell Crowe. There is one piece of evidence:

a fuzzy, early black and white photo of Russell knitting. Or at least, he's holding up some wool and needles in a somewhat unknitterly pose. Call me a cynic, but I found it hard to believe that a gladiatorial, alpha male like Crowe would knit, but then again, he has taken to quoting poetry . . .

I contact Russell's personal assistant, who promptly shoots back a denial. To quote:

Dear Sharon,
In answer to your questions:
No, the photo is not real. It has been very badly Photoshopped [that might account for the technique].
No, Russell doesn't knit.
But if that obviously fake picture encourages the neophyte knitters of the world, well . . . well good luck to them.

market.' John has been in the industry since 1975. 'I love it, I really do,' he says. 'It's creative. I love the colours, I love the textures, and it's tactile. It's a soft industry,' he says, 'nothing nasty about it. Most people who work in it love it.' They certainly love the new knitters.

'See the possibilities?' says John, holding out a crazy knit sample.

'Let me tell you first up,' says Heather joining him. 'Price is not bothering me—$12.95 retail a ball.'

'All our expensive yarns sold,' says John. 'If it's really good quality, people will buy.'

John and Heather are a good double act. They first worked together in the late 1980s, then Heather left to become a national buyer and subsequently ran her own business. Three years ago after a series of shake-ups in the industry Patons was brought back to Australia and John and Heather teamed up again. They've taken some risks including halving the range and are now starting to coordinate parts of the new line together. Today they're brimming with excitement, having just come back from the big European trade shows where the whole industry is abuzz. 'Everyone was so passionate,' says John, 'there's a particular gleam in their eyes. We have a guy in New Zealand who lives and breathes the business and he's been ringing us for years saying, "I think it's going to happen, I think it's going to happen."' John and Heather laugh. 'This time,' says John, 'I think he's finally right.'

'In the past knitting was a fashion follower,' says Heather, 'now it's a leader. I remember when I first saw the Ostrich range [Paton's very popular fluffy synthetic]. I rang John and said, "I've got to have it, I have to have it."'

'But this time it's very different,' agrees John. 'This time is a different type of knitting.'

'In the '80s it was very controlled,' says Heather, 'all "knit to patterns". This new generation will improvise. Today's young people think outside the square.'

'It's individual,' says John.

Their words are tumbling out on top of each other in their enthusiasm.

'It's got to be easy,' says John. 'There's low skill, high creativity, high desire to do things, which means we have to keep feeling the market.'

'But not something too onerous or too long term,' finishes Heather. 'That will put them off.'

For John and Heather the real challenge now is to convey this change to the shops where the presentations are often still focused towards the pattern and wool packs bond. 'It should be like going into a lolly shop with all these wonderful textures and colours,' says John. 'The young people are going in to see what they can create. You have to be able to say, "This is fashion, it's the end product, it's not a ball of yarn."' They remain disappointed with the imagery of many of the contemporary knitting books—'Still in the cowshed,' says John of the country twee affected in the photos.

'In our patterns we've been changing the imagery,' notes Heather, 'I've just done a book for teenagers with a screaming purple background. It's so important at the moment . . .' she says, 'to keep the trend going.' Heather designed the very popular scarf pattern book that kept selling out of woolshops and was given away at pub knitting. 'No abbreviations,' she says flicking through, 'show them the balls of yarn and then what they make.' The book was written in a handful of days when they realised how big the trend was. 'I knitted nine of the scarves,' she says, 'the girls in the office did the other four.'

They are, to say the least, thrilled by pub knitting. 'After the *Today Show* we went into a Spotlight store,' recounts John, 'and it was virtually yarn-free. The manager, who'd been sceptical, said, "We sell out everything we get in. It isn't a beat-up after all . . ."' Now says John, 'We're only just beginning, there's so much to do.' Next he's talking gifts, school programs with older knitters teaching younger.

'Crochet could be great,' says Heather bringing out a giant plastic crochet hook. They talk about their rivals.

'Nundle,' says John, 'those sort of people make it a better world.'

'It's not competition with us,' says Heather, 'it enhances and stimulates the entire business.'

'We keep breaking budget each month,' says John, 'the mills are working 24 hours a day and we still can't get enough out.'

———

Knitting, when it comes down to it is the new fashion, the new therapy, the new retro geek chic. It's the new black, the new yoga, the new lawn bowls and the new feminism. It's little bits of the new everything.

It makes us calmer. It makes us think. It makes us make things, so knitting makes us creative too. None of which is standard issue in our regular busy-dayed, got-to-get-ahead lives.

And because it's retro, knitting is also the new old. We are looking back at our heritage and our traditions, doing a bit of domestic archaeology and reclaiming grandma. The old skills, old crafts and old values are knocking off some of our hard corporate edges. None of this is new of course, but that is the point. In looking back as well as forward we're trying to become part of something that is bigger than just ourselves.

There is a photo in the Australian National Gallery of a woman standing outside a run-down tin hut. The earth around her is outback red, the sky outback blue. In the doorway is a blowsy blonde smoking a fag and behind her, a bloke boozing. But the woman stands there frozen, staring out in a red cocktail gown, with a flower in her hair and a face full of makeup. Later you notice that the hem on her dress has been ragged and slashed, but even that looks deliberate. The photo is part of a series by artist Tracey Moffattt entitled *Something More*. The image is sad, and more than a little malevolent, but still the woman keeps staring past the lens. Knitting too is something more. It's got something to do with wanting something more.

I keep thinking about all the knitters I've met. They're all staring out beyond their everyday realities too. Whether they're creating a big art concept like a house cosy that involves a swag of knitters and examines ideas of community, home and safety. Or whether their 'something more' is on a smaller scale: feral knitting without a pattern for the first time; refusing to stop knitting just because they're paralysed; seeing knitting as more than just technique; sitting alone for half an hour and avoiding all interruptions because they're working on their hobby; starting their own label to see in the markets; being determined that their child will wear at least one hand-knit garment. In hundred of ways, large and small, knitters are demanding more of themselves than just the normal, the everyday. More than the constant 'doing' of their regular lives.

Knitting and thinking. Slowing down. Time is our commodity now. We're as time poor as money poor. We hoard time, juggle it, trade off better pay to have more of it. The faster we have to run in the rest of our lives, the slower we want our hobbies. Radical for us, is spending time. Spending time knitting, spending time with our friends, spending time making gifts that would have been easier to buy. That's our benchmark of value. Our benchmark of sanity.

We're exhausted with our constant doing: doing the groovy career, the groovy clothes, the groovy look. Being a grown-up should be more fun than that. So knitting is also rebellious. The ultimate 'stuff you'. Dinner can wait, career can wait, the children can wait. Scary women waving needles saying, 'Go away, I'm knitting.'

So we sit, knit and think. The soft constant click of the needles, the repeat mantra knit one, purl one, knit one, purl one. Just sitting still. Just being. In our complicated juggling lives knitting is something so simple. Pick up a needle. Pick up some wool. Knit a stitch. Knit another. Just be. Stitch after stitch, fabric magically appears. We mould it, shape it, stitch it into something made only by our hands, two needles and some yarn.

And dammit, on top of all this, on top of the philosophy and the therapy and the creativity, more than anything knitting is just plain good fun.

So I can't help hoping that at least once next year I'll be sitting in the Cricketer's Arms, beer in one hand, knitting in the other, fending off another nostalgic Irish backpacker while shooting the breeze with some other mad knitter. It's party time.

Knitting patterns from Patons

Contents

Abbreviations

alt = alternate; **beg** = beginning; **cm** = centimetres; **cont** = continue; **dec** = decrease, decreasing; **foll** = follows, following; **garter st** = every row knit; **inc** = increase, increasing; **incl** = inclusive, including; **K** = knit; **0** (zero) = no sts, rows or times; **P** = purl; **patt** = pattern; **psso** = pass slipped st over; **purl fabric** (reverse stocking st) = 1 row purl (right side), 1 row knit (wrong side); **rem** = remain/ing; **rep** = repeat; **st/s** = stitch/es; **stocking st** = 1 row knit, 1 row purl; **sl** = slip; **tbl** = through back of loop; **tog** = together; **ybk** = yarn back (take yarn under needle from purling position into knitting position); **yfwd** = yarn forward (bring yarn under needle, then over into knitting position again, thus making a stitch); **yon** = yarn over needle (take yarn over top of needle into knitting position, thus making a stitch); **yrn** = yarn round needle (take yarn right round needle into purling position, thus making a stitch)

Scarves

Scarves are worked in the following easy stitches—

1   Garter stitch (every row knit)
2   stocking stitch (1 row knit, 1 row purl)
3   combinations of garter stitch and stocking stitch
4   1 × 1 rib
5   2 × 2 rib

Pattern instructions have been simplified and no abbreviations used.

As tension is not crucial to the finished size for a scarf, tensions have not been specified.

Changing the width or length

Each style gives a number of stitches to cast on and the approximate finished width. If you prefer a narrower or wider scarf, increase or decrease the number of stitches when casting on.

Changing the width is easy for garter stitch or stocking stitch. Where the pattern states to cast on 20 stitches and the finished approximate width is 20 cm, 1 stitch equals 1 cm. If you want your scarf to be 25 cm wide, just cast on 25 stitches.

When changing the width of rib scarves, the number of stitches must equal the rib pattern repeat.

- For 1 × 1 rib (1 knit stitch, then 1 purl stitch), the number of stitches cast on must be an *odd* number—as the repeat is 2 stitches (1 knit, then 1 purl) and 1 extra knit stitch is needed to 'even' up the rib.
- For 2 × 2 rib (2 knit stitches, then 2 purl stitches) the number of stitches cast on must be a multiple of 4, with 2 extra stitches added to 'even' up the rib. Possible stitch numbers to cast on for a 2 × 2 rib would be: 18, 22, 26, 30, 34 etc.

Ostrich and Feathers scarf, and easy cushion

Larger needles have been selected than usually recommended, so that scarves will be *quick* to knit. You can change the needle size; however, if smaller needles are used, your scarf will be narrower and if larger needles are used, your scarf will be wider.

Important—yarn quantity required
Changing the number of stitches cast on, scarf length or needle size will affect the quantity of yarn required. Be sure to purchase extra balls if changing any of these.

Ostrich and Feathers—stocking stitch

Approx. 20 cm width
1 ball Feathers and 1 ball Ostrich = approx. 48 cm length
2 balls Feathers and 2 balls Ostrich = approx. 96 cm length
3 balls Feathers and 3 balls Ostrich = approx. 144 cm length

Using 5.00 mm needles and Ostrich, cast on 40 stitches.
Using Ostrich—
1st row—Knit to end of row.
2nd row—Purl to end of row.
Last 2 rows form stocking stitch. Work 2 rows stocking stitch.
Change to Feathers.
Using Feathers, work 8 rows stocking stitch.
Last 12 rows form pattern—4 rows Ostrich, then 8 rows Feathers (all in stocking stitch).
Repeat pattern until scarf is desired length, ending with 4 rows Ostrich. Cast off.

Chunky fireside—2 × 2 rib

Approx. 11 cm width
2 balls Patons Fireside = approx. 70 cm length
4 balls Patons Fireside = approx. 140 cm length

Using 9 mm needles, cast on 22 stitches.
1st row—Knit 2 stitches, * Purl 2 stitches, Knit 2 stitches, repeat from * to end of row.
2nd row—Purl 2 stitches, * Knit 2 stitches, Purl 2 stitches, repeat from * to end of row.
Last 2 rows form 2 × 2 rib pattern.

Repeat 2 × 2 rib pattern until scarf measures desired length, ending with a 2nd row. Cast off.

Easy cushions

Measurements
Size (approx.) 35 × 35 cm

Yarn required
Patons Feathers 50 g balls—2
Patons Fireside 8 ply 50 g balls—2

Important! Use only the yarn specified for this cushion. Other yarns may give unsatisfactory results. Quantities are approximate as they can vary between knitters.

Accessories
1 pair each 4.50 mm (no. 9) and 4.00 mm (no. 8) knitting needles or sizes needed to give correct tension
35 × 35 cm cushion insert

Tension—18 sts and 24 rows to 10 cm over stocking st, using 4.50 mm needles and Feathers, and 22 sts and 30 rows to 10 cm over stocking st, using 4.00 mm needles and Fireside 8 ply. Please check your tension carefully. If less sts use smaller needles, if more sts use bigger needles.

Front
Using 4.50 mm needles and Feathers, cast on 65 sts.
Work in stocking st until work measures 35 cm from beg, ending with a purl row.
Cast off loosely.

Back
Using 4.00 mm needles and Fireside 8 ply, cast on 79 sts.
Work in stocking st until work measures 35 cm from beg, ending with a purl row.
Cast off loosely.

Make up
Do not press. Using Fireside 8 ply and back-stitch, join Front and Back pieces tog, along three sides. Join rem side after enclosing cushion insert.

Plain cushions

Measurements
Size (approx.) 35 × 35 cm

Yarn required
Ostrich 50 g balls—3
Totem 8 ply 50 g balls—2

Important! Use only the yarn specified for these cushions. Other yarns may give unsatisfactory results. Quantities are approximate as they can vary between knitters.

Accessories
1 pair 4.00 mm (no, 8) knitting needles or size needed to give correct tension
35 × 35 cm cushion insert

Tension—24 sts and 28 rows to 10 cm over stocking st, using 4.00 mm needles and Ostrich.
22 stsand 30 rows to 10 cm over stocking st, using 4.00 mm needles.
Please check your tension carefully. If less sts use smaller needles, if more sts use bigger needles.

Front
Using 4.00 mm needles and Ostrich, cast on 86 sts.
Work in stocking st until work measures 35 cm from beg, ending with a purl row.
Cast off loosely.

Back
Using 4.00 mm needles and Totem 8 ply, cast on 79 sts.
Work in stocking st until work measures 35 cm from beg, ending with a purl row.
Cast off loosely.

Make up
Do not press. Using Totem 8 ply and back-stitch, join Front and Back pieces tog along three sides. Join rem side after enclosing cushion insert.

Tea cosy

Yarn required
Patons Totem 8 ply 50 gm balls
1st colour (C1)—1
2nd colour (C2)—1

Accessories
1 pair 5.50 mm needles

Tension—18 sts to 10 cm over stocking st using yarn double.

Note: Yarn is worked double throughout.

Using 5.50 mm needles and C1 double, cast on 27 sts.
1st row—Knit (wrongside).
** **2nd row**—Knit.
3rd row—K1, purl to last 3 sts, K3.
Using C2—**4th row**—Knit to the last 2 sts, turn, (bring yarn to front of work slip 2nd last stitch from left hand needle to right hand needle, take yarn to back of work, slip 2nd last st back onto right hand needle) now turn your work, place left hand needle into right hand and right hand needle into left hand.
5th row—Knit.
Using C1 rep 2nd and 3rd rows once. **
Rep from ** to ** 7 times in all (carrying yarn not in use along bottom edge of work)
Using C1—**Next row**—Knit
Cast off.
Make another piece the same.

Make up
Using a flat seam sew the pieces tog at top on one side.
Using C2 knit up 34 sts along top of tea cosy.

Tea cosy, and garter stitch hot water bottle cover

1st row—Knit
2nd row—K2 tog . . . 17 sts.
Cast off knitways.
Join other side tog at top and both bottom seams allowing openings
to fit spout and handle of teapot.

Garter stitch hot water bottle cover

Measurements
Size (approx.) 21 × 36 cm

Yarn required
Fireside 8 ply 50 g balls
1st colour (C1)—2
2nd colour (C2)—2

Important! Use only the yarn specified for these items. Other yarns may give unsatisfactory results. Quantities are approximate as they can vary between knitters.

Accessories
1 pair each 3.75 mm (no. 9) and 3.00 mm (no. 11) knitting needles or sizes needed to give correct tension
A standard hot water bottle, measuring approx. 20 cm wide and 35 cm long

Tension—22.5 sts and 46 rows to 10 cm over garter st, using 3.75 mm needles. To work tension square, use 3.75 mm needles, cast on 33 sts. Knit 69 rows garter st. Cast off loosely. To achieve the desired effect, these items have been designed to be worked on smaller needles at a tighter tension than usually recommended. Please check your tension carefully. If less sts use smaller needles, if more sts use bigger needles.

Back and front (alike)—Using 3.75 mm Needles and C1, cast on 49 sts.
Knit 1 row (1st row is wrong side).
Knit 12 rows garter st, in stripes of 6 rows each C1 and C2.

These 12 rows form patt.

Cont in patt until work measures approx 27 cm from beg, ending with a complete C1 stripe.

Shape top—- Keeping stripes correct, cast off 3 sts at beg of next 6 rows . . . 31 sts.

Next row—K4, * inc in next st, K1, rep from * to last 3 sts, K3 . . . 43 sts.

Change to 3.00 mm Needles.

Beg rib—**1st row**—K1, * P1, K1, rep from * to end.

2nd row—K2, * P1, K1, rep from * to last st, K1.

Last 2 rows form rib patt.

Work 1 row.

Next row (eyelet row)—K2, * yfwd, K2tog, P1, K1, rep from * to last st, K1.

Work a further 17 rows rib, beg with a 1st row.

Cast off loosely in rib.

Make up

Using back-stitch, join cast-on edges and side seams. Using 4 strands of yarn, 300 cm long, make a twisted cord. Thread cord through eyelet holes, beg and ending at 2 centre front eyelets and tie. Using C1, make 2 small pom poms and attach to twisted cord.

Rib beanie

Yarn required

Patons 8 ply 50 gm balls

Main Colour (M)—2

Contrast Colour (C)—1

Accessories

1 pair 4.00 mm needles or size needed to give correct tension

Tension—22 sts and 30 rows to 10 cm over stocking st.

Using M and 4.00 mm needles cast on 73 sts.
1st row—K3, * P2, K3 rep from * to end.
2nd row—P3, * K2, P3 rep from * to end.
These 2 rows form rib pattern.
Cont in M until work measures 4.5 cm from beg.
Keeping rib correct—beg stripe pattern 4 rows C, 4 rows M, 4 rows C, using M for remainder cont in rib until work measures 15 cm from beg.
Shape Crown—**1st row**—K2, sl 1, K1, psso, rib 8, sl 1, K1, psso, rib 13, sl 1, K1, psso, rib 15, K2tog, rib 13, K2tog, rib 8, K2tog, K2 . . . 67 sts
2nd and alt rows—Knit all knit sts and purl all purl sts as they appear.
3rd row—K2, sl 1, K1, psso, rib 7, sl 1, K1, psso, rib 12, sl 1, K1, psso, rib 13, K2tog, rib 12, K2tog, rib 7, K2tog, K2 . . . 61 sts
5th row—K2, sl 1, K1, psso, rib 6, sl 1, K1, psso, rib 11, sl 1, K1, psso, rib 11, K2tog, rib 11, K2tog, rib 6 , K2tog, K2 . . . 55 sts
7th row—K2, sl 1, K1, psso, rib 5, sl 1, K1, psso, rib 10, sl 1, K1, psso, rib 9, K2tog, rib 10, K2tog, rib 5, K2tog, K2 . . . 49 sts
9th row—K2, sl 1, K1, psso, rib 4, sl 1, K1, psso, rib 9, sl 1, K1, psso, rib 7, K2tog, rib 9, K2tog, rib 4, K2tog, K2 . . . 43 sts
11th row—K2, sl 1, K1, psso, rib 3, sl 1, K1, psso, rib 8, sl 1, K1, psso, rib 5, K2tog, rib 8, K2tog, rib 3, K2tog, K2 . . . 37 sts.
13th row—K2, sl 1, K1, psso, rib 2, sl 1, K1, psso, rib 7, sl 1,K1, psso, rib3, K2tog, rib 7, K2tog, rib 3, K2tog, K2 . . . 31 sts.
15th row—K2, sl 1, K1, psso, K1, sl 1, K1, psso, rib 6, sl 1, K1, psso, K1, K2tog, rib 6, K2tog, K1, K2tog, K2 . . . 25 sts.

Chunky fireside scarf, rib beanie, and basket stitch dog coat

17th row—K2, (sl 1, K1, psso) twice, rib 5, sl 1, K2tog, psso, rib 5, (K2tog) twice, K2 . . . 19 sts.

19th row—K2, sl 2, K1, psso, rib 3, sl 1, K2tog, psso, rib 3, K2tog, K2 . . . 13 sts.

20th row—As 2nd row.

Cast off in rib.

Make another piece.

Make up

Using back-stitch and right sides together join side and top seams together.

Basket stitch dog coat

Measurements

Size		XXS	XS	S	M
Width (approx.)	cm	23	28	33	38
	ins	9	11	13	15
Length (approx. —incl. buttonholes)	cm	19	32	45	58

Yarn required

Courtelle 8 ply 100 g balls

Important! Use only the yarn specified for this dog coat. Other yarns may give unsatisfactory results. Quantities are approximate as they can vary between knitters.

Accessories

1 pair each 4.00 mm (no. 8) and 3.25 mm (no. 10) knitting needles or sizes needed to give correct tension

3.50 mm (no. 10–11) crochet hook

2 (3-3-4) buttons

Tension—21 sts and 36 rows to 10 cm over patt, using 4.00 mm needles. To work tension square use 4.00 mm needles, cast on 30 sts.

Work 58 rows patt. Cast off loosely.

Please check your tension carefully. If less sts use smaller needles, if more sts use bigger needles.

Dog coat

Using 4.00 mm needles, cast on 50 (**62-70-82**) sts.

1st row—K2, * P2, K2, rep from * to end.

2nd row—P2, * K2, P2, rep from * to end.

3rd row—As 2nd row.

4th row—As 1st row.

Rows 1 to 4 incl form patt.

Cont in patt until work measures 15 (**23-31-39**) cm (or length desired) from beg, working last row on wrong side.

Shape neck—**Next row**—Patt 16 (**21-24-29**), cast off next 18 (**20-22-24**) sts, patt to end.

** Cont on last 16 (**21-24-29**) sts.

Dec at neck edge in every (**every-alt-4th**) rows until 8 (**19-21-26**) sts rem, then in foll alt (**alt-4th-6th**) rows until 6 (**10-13-18**) sts rem.
**

Work 11 rows patt.

Cast off.

With wrong side facing, join yarn to rem sts.

Rep from ** to **.

Work 5 rows patt.

Size XXS only—6th row—Patt 2, cast off 2 sts, patt 2.

7th row—Patt 2, **turn**, cast on 2 sts, **turn**, patt 2 . . . buttonhole.

Sizes XS, S and M only—6th row—Patt 2 (**3-3**), cast off 2 sts, [patt 2 (**3-3**), cast off 2 sts] 1 (**1-2**) time/s, patt 2 (**3-3**).

7th row—Patt 2 (**3**-**3**), **turn**, cast on 2 sts, **turn**, [patt 2 (**3**-**3**), **turn**, cast on 2 sts, **turn**] 1 (**1**-**2**) time/s, patt 2 (**3**-**3**) . . . 2 (**2**-**3**) buttonholes.
All sizes—Work 4 rows patt.
Cast off.

Strap
Using 3.25 mm needles, cast on 7 sts.
1st row—K2, (P1, K1) twice, K1.
2nd row—K1, (P1, K1) 3 times.
Rep 1st and 2nd rows until strap measures 15 (**19**-**23**-**27**) cm (or length desired) from beg, ending with a 2nd row.
Next row—Rib 3, cast off 2 sts, rib 2.
Next row—Rib 2, **turn**, cast on 2 sts, **turn**, rib 3 . . . buttonhole.
Work 4 rows rib.
Cast off in rib.

Make up
Do not press. Using 3.50 mm hook, work 1 row dc evenly around all outer edges and working 3dc in every corner, omitting strap. Sew strap to coat 7 (**13**-**19**-**25**) cm from cast-on edge. Sew on buttons to match buttonholes.

Baby's Hat, Bootees and Headband

Measurements

Approx age	months	0	3	6	12	18
Hat (approx. fits head)	cm	35	40	45	50	52.5
	ins	14	16	18	20	21
Bootees (approx. fits foot)	cm	8		9.5		
	ins	3		4		

Baby's bootees and headband

Yarn required
Patons Dreamtime 4 ply 25 g balls

Plain hat	2	2	2	3	3

Bootees

Main Colour (M)	1	1	1	1	1
Contrast Colour (C)	1	1	1	1	1

Headband

Main Colour (M)	1	1	1	1	1
Contrast Colour (C)	Small quantity				

Important! Use only the yarn specified for these garments. Other yarns may give unsatisfactory results. Quantities are approximate as they vary between knitters.

Accessories
1 pair each 3.25 mm (no. 10) and 2.75 mm (no. 12) knitting needles or sizes needed to give correct tension

Tension—28 sts and 38.5 rows to 10 cm over stocking st, using 3.25 mm needles. Please work your tension square as follows: Using 3.25 mm needles, cast on 42 sts. Work 52 rows stocking st. Cast off loosely.
Please check your tension carefully. If less sts use smaller needles, if more sts use bigger needles.

Plain hat
Using 3.25 mm needles, cast on 113 (**129**-141-**151**-157) sts.
1st row—K1, * P1, K1, rep from * to end.
2nd row—K2, * P1, K1, rep from * to last st, K1.
Rep 1st and 2nd rows 9 times, then 1st row once . . . 21 rows rib in all.
Change to 3.25 mm needles.

Work in stocking st (beg with a knit row—thus reversing fabric) until work measures 8 (9-10-11-12) cm from **centre** of rib, ending with a purl row and dec 0 (0-4-6-4) sts evenly across last row . . . 113 (**129-137-145**-153) sts.

Shape crown—**1st row**—K1, * K2tog, K12 (**14-15-16**-17), rep from * to end . . . 105 (**121-129-137**-145) sts.

Work 3 rows.

5th row—K1, * K2tog, K11 (**13-14-15**-16), rep from * to end . . . 97 (**113-121-129**-137) sts.

Work 3 rows.

9th row—K1, * K2tog, K10 (**12-13-14**-15), rep from * to end . . . 89 (**105-113-121**-129) sts.

Work 3 rows.

13th row—K1, * K2tog, K9 (**11-12-13**-14), rep from * to end . . . 81 (**97-105-113**-121) sts.

Work 3 rows.

17th row—K1, * K2tog, K8 (**10-11-12**-13), rep from * to end . . . 73 (**89-97-105**-113) sts.

Work 1 row.

19th row—K1, * K2tog, rep from * to end . . . 37 (**45-49-53**-57) sts.

Work 1 row.

21st row—K1, * K2tog, rep from * to end . . . 19 (**23-25-27**-29) sts. Break off yarn. Run end through rem sts, draw up tightly and fasten off securely.

Make up

With a slightly damp cloth and warm iron (unless stated otherwise on ball band), press lightly on wrong side. Using back-stitch, join seam, noting to reverse seam for brim. Fold brim onto right side for half of rib rows.

Bootees (beg at sole)

Using 3.25 mm needles and M, cast on 31 (39) sts.
1st row—[Inc in next st, K13 (17), inc in next st] twice, K1.
2nd and alt rows—Knit.
3rd row—[Inc in next st, K15 (19), inc in next st] twice, K1.
5th row—[Inc in next st, K17 (21), inc in next st] twice, K1.
7th row—[Inc in next st, K19 (23), inc in next st] twice, K1.
9th row—[Inc in next st, K21 (25), inc in next st] twice, K1 . . .
51 (59) sts.
Work 15 rows stocking st, beg with a purl row.
Shape instep—**1st row**—K30 (34), sl 1 knitways, K1, psso, **turn.**
2nd row—P10, P2tog, **turn.**
3rd row—K10, sl 1 knitways, K1, psso, **turn.**
4th row—P10, P2tog, **turn.**
5th row—K10, sl 1 knitways, K1, psso, **turn.**
Rep 2 to 5 incl 2 (3) times, then 2nd row once.
Next row—Knit to end . . . 37 (41) sts.
Work 13 rows stocking st, beg with a purl row.
Change to 2.75 mm needles.
Using C, knit 6 rows garter st.
Cast off loosely.

Bow

Using 2.75 mm needles and C, cast on 15 sts.
Knit 14 rows garter st (1st row is wrong side).
Cast off knitways.

Make up

With a slightly damp cloth and warm iron (unless stated otherwise on ball band), press lightly on wrong side. Using back-stitch, join leg seam. Using a flat seam, join foot seam. Make 2 bows, gather centre of bow, winding yarn around and attach to front of each bootee.

Headband

Using 3.25 mm needles and M, cast on 7 sts.

Knit in garter st until work measures 40 cm (or length desired) from beg.

Cast off loosely knitways.

Using a flat seam, join ends together.

Bow

Using 2.75 mm needles and C, cast on 15 sts.

Knit 14 rows garter st (1st row is wrong side).

Cast off knitways.

Gather centre of bow, winding yarn around, then sew bow to centre of headband.

Crew sweater in 4 ply

Measurements

This garment is designed to be a generous fit.

Months		0	3	6	12
Fits underarm	cm	35	40	45	50
Garments measure	**cm**	**41**	**48**	**54**	**60**
Length	cm	23	26	29	33
Sleeve fits	cm	11	13	16	19

Yarn required

Dreamtime 4 ply 25 g balls

	4	5	6	7

Important! Use only the yarn specified for these garments. Other yarns may give unsatisfactory results. Quantities are approximate as they can vary between knitters.

Accessories

1 pair each 3.25 mm (no. 10) and 2.75 mm (no. 12) knitting
needles or sizes needed to give correct tension
2 stitch holders
2 buttons for shoulder opening
If desired, purchased motif

Tension—27 sts and 55 rows to 10 cm over garter st, using
3.25 mm needles. To work tension square, use 3.25mm Needles,
cast on 39 sts. Knit 81 rows garter st. Cast off loosely.
Please check your tension carefully. If less sts use smaller needles, if
more sts use bigger needles.

Back

Using 3.25 mm needles, cast on 57 (67-75-83) sts.
Knit in garter st (1st row is wrong side) until work measures
22 (25-28-32) cm from beg, working last row on wrong side.
Shape shoulders—Cast off 5 (7-8-9) sts at beg of next 4 rows, then
6 (7-8-9) sts at beg of foll 2 rows.
Leave rem 25 (25-27-29) sts on a stitch-holder.

Front

Work as for Back until work measures 5 (5-5-5.5) cm **less** than
Back to beg of shoulder shaping, working last row on wrong side.
Shape neck—**Next row**—K23 (28-31-35), **turn.**
** Cont on these 23 (28-31-35) sts.
Dec at neck edge in alt rows until 18 (23-26-29) sts rem, then in
foll 4th rows until 16 (21-24-27) sts rem.
Cont without shaping until work measures same as Back to beg of
shoulder shaping, working last row on wrong side.
Shape shoulder—Cast off 5 (7-8-9) sts at beg of next row and foll
alt row. Work 1 row. Cast off rem 6 (7-8-9) sts. **
Slip next 11 (11-13-13) sts onto stitch-holder and leave.

Join yarn to rem sts and knit to end.

Rep from ** to **, working 1 row more before shoulder shaping.

Sleeves

Using 3.25 mm needles, cast on 37 (**39-41-43**) sts.

Knit in garter st (1st row is wrong side), inc at each end of 3rd row and foll 6th rows until there are 51 (**57-63-65**) sts, then in foll 8th row/s until there are 53 (**59-65-71**) sts.

Cont without shaping until work measures 11 (**13-16-19**) cm (or length desired) from beg, working last row on wrong side.

Cast off loosely knitways.

Neckband

Using back-stitch, join right shoulder seam. With right side facing and using 2.75 mm needles, knit up 14 (**14-14-15**) sts evenly along left side of neck, knit across sts from front stitch-holder, knit up 14 (**14-14-15**) sts evenly along right side of neck, then knit across sts from back stitch-holder . . . 64 (**64-68-72**) sts.

Knit 7 rows garter st.

Cast off loosely knitways.

Make up

Do not press. Using back-stitch, join left shoulder for 2 cm. Tie coloured threads 10 (**11-12-13**) cm down from beg of shoulder shaping on side edges of Back and Fronts to mark armholes. Sew in sleeves evenly between coloured threads, placing centre of sleeves to shoulder seams. Join side and sleeve seams. Using a hook, work 1 round dc evenly around left shoulder opening, making two 3ch buttonloops evenly along back shoulder. Sew on buttons. Stitch motif in place if desired.

Jackets with options in 4 ply

Measurements
These garments are designed to be a generous fit.

Months		0	3	6	12
Fits underarm	cm	35	40	45	50
Garments measure	**cm**	**41**	**48**	**54**	**60**
Length	cm	23	26	29	33
Sleeve fits (with cuff turned back)	cm	11	13	16	19

Yarn required
Dreamtime 4 ply 25 g balls

	0	3	6	12
Crew Button Jacket	5	6	7	8
Hood Button Jacket	7	8	9	10

Important! Use only the yarn specified for these garments. Other yarns may give unsatisfactory results. Quantities are approximate as they can vary between knitters.

Accessories
1 pair each 3.25 mm (no. 10) and 2.75 mm (no. 12) knitting needles or sizes needed to give correct tension
1 stitch holder for Crew Button Jacket and purchased ribbon roses
Purchased motif for Hood Button Jacket
3 Buttons

Tension—27 sts and 55 rows to 10 cm over garter st, using 3.25 mm needles. To work tension square, use 3.25 mm needles, cast on 39 sts. Knit 75 rows garter st. Cast off loosely.

Please check your tension carefully. If less sts use smaller needles, if more sts use bigger needles.

Crew button jacket

Back
Using 3.25 mm needles, cast on 57 (67-75-83) sts.
Knit in garter st (1st row is wrong side) until work measures
22 (25-28-32) cm from beg, working last row on wrong side.
Shape shoulders—Cast off 5 (7-8-9) sts at beg of next 4 rows, then
6 (7-8-9) sts at beg of foll 2 rows.
Leave rem 25 (25-27-29) sts on stitch-holder.

Left front
Using 3.25 mm needles, cast on 28 (33-37-41) sts.
Knit in garter st (1st row is wrong side) until work measures
5 (5-5-5.5) cm **less** than Back to beg of shoulder shaping, ending
with a wrong side row. **
Work 1 row.
Shape neck—**Next row**—Cast off 6 (6-7-7) sts, knit to end . . .
22 (27-30-34) sts.
*** Dec at neck edge in next and alt rows until 19 (24-27-30) sts
rem, then in foll 4th rows until 16 (21-24-27) sts rem.
Cont without shaping until work measures same as Back to beg of
shoulder shaping, working last row on wrong side.
Shape shoulder—Cast off 5 (7-8-9) sts at beg of next row and foll
alt row. Work 1 row. Cast off rem 6 (7-8-9) sts. ***

Right front
Work as for Left Front to **.
Shape neck—**Next row**—Cast off 6 (6-7-7) sts, knit to end . . .
22 (27-30-34) sts.
Work 1 row.
Work as for Left Front from *** to ***, working 1 row more
before shoulder shaping.

Sleeves
Using 3.25 mm needles, cast on 37 (39-41-43) sts.
Knit in garter st (1st row is wrong side) until work measures
4 (4-5-5) cm from beg, working last row on wrong side.
Tie a coloured thread at each end of last row to mark end of cuff.
Change to 2.75 mm needles.
Cont in garter st, inc at each end of 3rd row and foll 6th rows
4 (4-5-5) times in all . . . 45 (47-51-53) sts.
Change to 3.25 mm needles.
Cont in garter st, inc at each end of foll 6th rows until there
are 51 (57-63-65) sts, then in foll 8th row/s until there are
53 (59-65-71) sts.
Cont without shaping until work measures 11 (13-16-19) cm (or
length desired) from coloured threads, working last row on wrong
side.
Cast off loosely knitways.

Neckband
Using back-stitch, join shoulder seams. With right side facing and
using 2.75 mm needles, knit up 20 (20-21-22) sts evenly along right
side of neck, knit across sts from back stitch-holder, then knit up
20 (20-21-22) sts evenly along left side of neck . . . 65 (65-69-73) sts.
Knit 5 rows garter st.
Cast off loosely knitways.

Right front band
With right side facing and using 2.75 mm needles, knit up 53 (61-
69-79) sts evenly along right front edge and side edge of neckband.
Knit 2 rows garter st.
3rd row—K3, cast off 2 sts, [K7 (7-9-11), cast off 2 sts] twice, knit
to end.
4th row—Knit to last 17 (17-21-25) sts, **turn**, cast on 2 sts, **turn**,
[K7 (7-9-11, **turn**, cast on 2 sts, **turn**] twice, K3 . . . 3 buttonholes.

Knit 1 row garter st.

Cast off loosely knitways.

Left front band

Work to correspond with Right Front Band, omitting buttonholes.

Make up

Do not press. Tie coloured threads 10 (**11-12-13**) cm down from beg of shoulder shaping on side edges of Back and Fronts to mark armholes. Sew in sleeves evenly between coloured threads, placing centre of sleeves to shoulder seams. Join side and sleeve seams, reversing seam for rows below coloured threads for cuffs. Turn back cuffs onto right side. Sew on buttons. Attach ribbon roses as pictured.

Hood button jacket

Back, left and right fronts and sleeves

Work as for **Crew Button Jacket,** noting to cast off sts at back neck.

Right front band

Using back-stitch, join shoulder seams. With right side facing and using 2.75 mm needles, knit up 53 (**61-69-79**) sts evenly along right front edge.

Knit 2 rows garter st.

3rd row—K3, cast off 2 sts, [K7 (**7-9-11**), cast off 2 sts] twice, knit to end.

4th row—Knit to last 17 (**17-21-25**) sts, **turn,** cast on 2 sts, **turn,** [K7 (**7-9-11, turn,** cast on 2 sts, **turn**] twice, K3 . . . 3 buttonholes.

Knit 1 row garter st.

Cast off loosely knitways.

Left front band

Work to correspond with Right Front Band, omitting buttonholes.

Hood

Using 3.25 mm needles, cast on 85 (85-97-101) sts.

Knit in garter st (1st row is wrong side) until work measures 18 (19-20-21) cm (or length desired) from beg, working last row on wrong side.

Cast off loosely.

Make up

Do not press. Tie coloured threads 10 (11-12-13) cm down from beg of shoulder shaping on side edges of Back and Fronts to mark armholes. Sew in sleeves evenly between coloured threads, placing centre of sleeves to shoulder seams. Join side and sleeve seams, reversing seam for rows below coloured threads for cuffs. Turn back cuffs onto right side. Fold hood in half lengthwise and using back-stitch, join top of hood (cast-off edge) tog, reversing seam for 4 (4-5-5) cm. Turn back brim for 4 (4-5-5) cm and stitch in place. Sew cast-on edge of hood evenly around neck edge, sewing through both thicknesses of brim and easing to fit. Sew on buttons.

Acknowledgements

No book like this gets written without an awful lot of people giving you their time. Knitters universally did this without question and I didn't meet one I didn't like. My gratitude to all my interview subjects: your stories were all wonderful. Special thanks too to interviewees who haven't been quoted in the final draft. Your ideas are there, even if your name isn't. A big thank you to:

John Albert, Adele Anderson, Amy Barker, Karen Bateman, Marta Cantos, Jo Carswell, Fiona Cleverly, Carol Collier, Aoife Clifford, Kelley Deal, Audrey Dixon, Tania Djipalo, Amanda Ducker, Marion East, Emma Eaton, Edith Eig, Sabina Finnern, Robyn Fallick, David Flynn, Sue Flynn, Gloria Fong, Liz Gemmell, Eva Gerencer, Greta Gergely, Sonia Gidley-King, Germaine Goh, Heather Granger, Sue Green, Donyale Harrison, Joy Harrison, Lisa Herrod, Judy Howarth, Michael Hurley, Tiffany Hutton, Sue Jardin, Peter Jopson, Clare Kendall, Kerrie-Anne, Kirsten Krauth, Sophie Lee, Louise Loomes, Mac, John Macarthur, Tom Moore, Val Moreley, Albert Morris, Rebecca Mostyn, Nikki Mumford, Kate Nash, Claire Patterson, Jo Paul, Pia Seeto, Jo Sharp, Frances Stone, Val Quarmby, Margaret Reid, Lisa Ryan,

Marianne Saliba, Bronwyn Sandland, Jeanette Shennan, Shona Smith, Susannah, Geraldine Thumboo, Sally Tulloch, Danni Townsend, Linley Valente, Mary Helen Ward, Ann Westin, Joanne Yates.

The knitting patterns and instructions have been generously provided by Patons, for which I am much indebted.

No book gets written well without editors and here I couldn't have wished for better. Many thanks firstly to Jo Paul who commissioned the book, cheered me on, took me to lunch and kept me and my ideas on track. Secondly to Colette Vella, who took a jungle of a first draft and found a clear path— my book is better for it. And finally to my husband Rob Johnson, who read more drafts than he could have wished for and always made them better.

References

'Australia's Place in the Global Wool Industry—Scoping Study', 2001, A report prepared for Australian Wool Innovation P/L

Blainey, Geoffrey, 1980 *A Land Half Won*, Macmillan, Melbourne

Braverman, Harry, 1975 *Labor and Monopoly Capital: the degradation of work in the twentieth century*, Monthly Review Press, New York

Clark, C.M.H., 1962 *A History of Australia*, vol. 1, Melbourne University Press, Melbourne

Gordon Lydon, Susan, 1997 *The Knitting Sutra*, Harpers, San Francisco, USA

Harvey, Michael, 1985 *Patons, A Story of Handknitting*, Little Hills Press, Sydney

Horwitz, Tess, 1997 Introductory essay to Marion East's exhibition *Shadow of a Dog* (Woolf letter, quoted in chapter one of this book)

Minwel Tibbott, S. 1978 'Knitting stockings in Wales—A domestic craft', in *Folk Life, A Journal of Ethnological Studies*, ed. by J. Geraint Jenkins, vol. 16

Mitchell, Kirk, 2001 'Knitting encourages inmates' needling', *Denver Post*, Monday November 26

Moore, Tom, 2002 'Beyond Technique' *The Australian Hand Weaver and Spinner*, vol. 55

'Slumber Party', 2002 *Sydney Morning Herald*, 21 June

Rogers, Jerry, 1991 *The Art of Knitting*, Angus & Robertson, North Ryde, Sydney

Rutt, Richard, 1987 *A History of Handknitting*, Interweave Press, Loveland, Colorado USA

Woolf, Virginia, 1987 *A Room of One's Own*, Triad Grafton, London